DISCO

INSIDE ISSUE 5: EXODUS, ACTS, JOHN

1 Find a time when you can read the Bible each day

2 Find a place where you can be quiet and think

4 Ask God to help you understand what you read

3 Grab your Bible and a pencil or pen

5 Read today's Discover page and Bible bit

6 Pray about what you have read and learned

We want to...

- Explain the Bible clearly to you
- Help you enjoy your Bible
- Encourage you to turn to Jesus
- Help Christians follow Jesus

Discover stands for...

- Total commitment to God's Word, the Bible
- Total commitment to getting its message over to you

Team Discover

Martin Cole, Nicole Carter, Rachel Jones, Kirsty McAllister, Alison Mitchell, André Parker, Ben Woodcraft

Discover is published by The Good Book Company, Blenheim House, 1 Blenheim Rd, Epsom, Surrey, KT19 9AP, UK.

Tel: 0333 123 0880; Email: discover@thegoodbook.co.uk UK: thegoodbook.co.uk

North America: thegoodbook.com   Australia: thegoodbook.com.au   NZ: thegoodbook.co.nz

How to use Discover

Here at Discover, we want you at home to get the most out of reading the Bible. It's how God speaks to us today. And He's got loads of top things to say.

We use the New International Version (NIV) of the Bible. You'll find that the NIV and New King James Version are best for doing the puzzles in Discover.

The Bible has 66 different books in it. So if the notes say…

Read Exodus 1 v 1

…turn to the contents page of your Bible and look down the list of books to see what page Exodus begins on. Turn to that page.

"Exodus 1 v 1" means you need to go to chapter 1 of Exodus, and then find verse 1 of chapter 1 (the verse numbers are the tiny ones). Then jump in and read it!

Here's some other stuff you might come across…

WEIRD WORDS

Chumkah
These boxes explain baffling words or phrases we come across in the Bible.

Think!

This bit usually has a tricky personal question on what you've been reading about.

Action!

Challenges you to put what you've read into action.

Wow!

This section contains a gobsmacking fact that sums up what you've been reading about.

Pray!

Gives you ideas for prayer. Prayer is talking to God. Don't be embarrassed! You can pray in your head if you want to. God still hears you! Even if there isn't a Pray! symbol, it's a good idea to pray about what you've read anyway.

Coming up in Issue 5...

Exodus: God to the rescue

At the start of the book of Exodus things are pretty miserable for God's people, the Israelites: they're slaves in Egypt, forced to make bricks all day, and now the King of Egypt is trying to kill all their baby boys!

But God has a plan to rescue his people. It involves one *very* scared Israelite leader (Moses) and one *very* stubborn Egyptian King (Pharaoh).

Cue one of the greatest showdowns in history! "God v Pharaoh" is a match with ten terrifying rounds, millions of gross insects and a BIG message we all need to hear: God is more powerful than anyone else and will rescue his people no matter what!

Acts: Gospel gets around

We pick up the book of Acts about halfway through. Way back in chapter 1 Jesus told his followers to take the good news to the ends of the earth—and now Paul and his companions are travelling further and further to do exactly that!

Everywhere Paul goes, he tells people the gospel—the good news that Jesus died for our sins and was raised back to life. Some people believe the message and follow Jesus. Other people reject it and try to stop his followers. In either case, life on the road with Paul is definitely never boring!

John: Word on the street

The book of John was written by (you guessed it!) a guy called John. He was one of the 12 disciples who spent years travelling with Jesus, listening to his teaching and watching him do amazing miracles. And then John wrote a book about it!

Why? Because John wants us to believe that Jesus is God's Son, sent to rescue us from sin and offer us eternal life.

So watch what happens when Jesus turns up at a wedding, sit in on an EPIC picnic and find out why Jesus trashed the temple and got away with it!

Psalms: Songs to God

Warm up your vocal chords and grab a microphone as we dive into Psalms—a book of songs. (The P is silent, it rhymes with "arms"!)

Lots of the Psalms were written by King David. But these aren't the sort of songs you'll hear on the radio any time soon—they don't rhyme and they're definitely NOT about David's girlfriend! The Psalms are about how great God is and what it looks like to trust him, whether things are going well or badly. Which means they're great songs for us to read and sing in our hearts too!

Time to turn up the volume and turn over the page...

Exodus: God to the rescue

*We kick off
this issue with
an excellent
examination of
Exodus.*

*It's the story of
God's people, the
Israelites.*

*And how God
rescued them
from Egypt.*

*But first, a bit of
history...*

WEIRD WORDS

Israel
Here it's another
name for Jacob,
Joseph's dad

**Exceedingly
fruitful**
The Israelites had
lots of babies, so
there were lots of
Israelites!

Exodus is the second book in
the Bible. So we'd better remind
ourselves what happened in the first
book, Genesis.

The Bible so far...

- God created everything, including
  people!

- But Adam and Eve disobeyed God.
  They brought sin into the world
  and messed up God's perfect
  creation.

- People became so sinful that God
  sent a terrible flood to punish
  them. Only Noah's family survived.

God made three amazing promises
to Abraham and his descendants,
the Israelites:

- They would become a huge
  NATION.

- He'd give them the **LAND** of
  Canaan to live in.

- All nations will be **BLESSED**
  through one of Abraham's
  descendants (Jesus).

- The Israelites did live in Canaan for
  a while.

- But a famine made them move to
  Egypt, where Joseph was second
  in command.

- So the Israelites were now living in
  Egypt, outside the land God had
  promised them (Canaan).

Read Exodus 1 v 1-5

*How many Israelites were
there when they moved to
Egypt (v5)?*

Read verses 6-7

At the start of Exodus, Joseph and
his brothers have died. But look how
many Israelites there are now (v7)!
Loads!

Wow!

God had promised that the
Israelites would become a
great NATION. And He's keeping
His promise. God always keeps
His promises!

But what about God's promise
that they would live in Canaan? It's
not looking so good now they're
all stuck in Egypt. Well, Exodus is
all about God rescuing His people
from Egypt.

Pray!

*Dear God, thank you for the book
of Exodus. As I read about your
people, the Israelites, please teach
me how I can serve you more.
Amen.*

2

The Israelites in Egypt were growing more and more in number.

WEIRD WORDS

Shrewdly
Harshly and cleverly

Oppress them
Rule them cruelly

Forced labour
Making them do really hard work

Store cities
Where food was stored up

Ruthlessly
Cruelly

Hebrew
Israelite

Vigorous
Give birth quickly

Unfair-o

But life was about to get much harder for them...

Read Exodus 1 v 8-14

A new Pharaoh was put in charge of Egypt. He was worried that the Israelites would grow to be too powerful, and join forces with his enemies. So he made them slaves, forcing them to do back-breaking work. They were treated very cruelly.

What was the result of all this? To find out, put the blocks in the correct order. Then check v12.

The mor	aelites	d the more
y treate	nd spread	they mul
were badl	e the Isr	tiplied a

The mor		

Read verses 15-21

To stop the Israelites growing further, Pharaoh ordered the midwives to murder all baby boys that were born. Disgusting.

But what did the midwives do? (v17)

_____

_____

God has told us to obey people in authority (check out Romans 13 v 1). But there are times when we must disobey them. But only if we're told to do something which is disobeying God.

Think of some examples...

If we're told to lie

God gave the midwives children of their own! And He let the Israelite nation keep growing, despite the cruel Egyptians!

Pray!

Thank God that He looks after His people. Ask Him to give you the courage to stand up to things that are wrong.

3

Exodus 2 v 1-10

Pharaoh was worried about the huge number of Israelites living in Egypt.

He was determined to keep them under control and treat them cruelly.

WEIRD WORDS

Levite
From the family of Joseph's brother, Levi

Papyrus
Grass-like plant

Tar and pitch
Gloopy stuff used to make the basket waterproof

Hebrew
Israelite

It's a boy!

Fill in Pharaoh's sickening command from Exodus 1 v 22.

Now read Exodus 2 v 1-2

Imagine how these parents felt when they saw their baby was a boy! You can't hide a little baby for very long; his crying would give him away. So the baby's mum came up with a plan...

Read verses 3-10
Now fill in the facts!

> The baby was hidden for _____ months (v2)

> He was put in a b_____ and left in the reeds by the r_____ (v3)

> Rescued by Pharaoh's d_____ (v5)

> Amazingly, she asked the baby's m_____ to look after him! (v8)

> When the baby grew older, he became the s_____ of Pharaoh's daughter. She named him M_____ (v10)

Baby Moses was protected by an Egyptian! God can use the most unlikely people to carry out His perfect plans.

Wow!

God's enemies (like Pharaoh) try to attack and destroy God's people. But God is in control. He will never let His people be destroyed (Hebrews 13 v 5-6).

No matter what happens to them, God's people will never be wiped out. In fact, they will survive for ever with God!

Pray!

Thank God that He's with His people, even through the toughest times. Thank Him that the devil can't destroy God's people, Christians!

4

Moses in training

But **Moses** was no ordinary kid. He would grow up to be an important part of God's plan for His people. Today we're going to jump forward to the book of Acts (near the end of the Bible) to learn more about Moses.

So a baby has been born in Egypt.

Big deal — doesn't that happen all the time?

Read Acts 7 v 17-19

What time was getting nearer (v17)? Go backwards one letter to find out (B=A, C=B, D=C etc).

___ ____
U I F   U J N F

___ ____ __
G P S   H P E   U P

_____
G V M G J M I J T

_____ __
Q S P N J T F   U P

_____
B C S B I B N

God promised Abraham that his descendants (the Israelites) would live freely in the land of Canaan, not as slaves in Egypt. As the time got nearer, God started preparing Moses for his part in God's rescue plan.

Treacherously
Betraying them

Oppressed
Ruled over them cruelly

Read verses 20-23

Moses was born (v20)

Despite being an Israelite, he was brought up in Pharaoh's palace (v21)

Moses did very well at school in Egypt (v22)

Moses lived in Egypt for 40 years! But he still cared about his people, the Israelites (v23)

Moses had an unusual upbringing. But God was preparing him for the amazing work He had planned for him. And Moses didn't even know it!

Wow!

God wants all of His people to serve Him with their lives. And He gives us all different abilities. Some people are brainy, others are great at talking to people. Others are good at doing the little jobs many people hate. Ask God to train you up to serve Him!

5

Moses the murderer

Moses was a Hebrew (Israelite), but he'd been brought up in Pharaoh's palace.

One day he went to see how badly the Hebrew slaves were being treated.

WEIRD WORDS

Labour
Work

Hebrew
Israelite, one of God's people

Foreigner
Someone living in a foreign country

Read Exodus 2 v 11-22

Number the events in the order they happened.

(1) Moses saw an Egyptian beating up a Hebrew

( ) There he rescued 7 sisters from some shepherds

( ) The man said, "You can't tell me what to do! Or will you kill me too?"

( ) So Moses ran away to Midian

( ) Moses married Zipporah and they had a son

( ) The next day Moses stopped two Hebrews who were fighting

( ) Pharaoh heard that Moses had killed an Egyptian and so wanted to kill Moses

( ) Their father invited Moses for a meal

( ) He killed the Egyptian and hid the body

I thought God was going to use Moses to rescue the Hebrews from Egypt. But now he's a murderer who has run away from Egypt!

God often uses weak, sinful people in His amazing plans! Moses had messed up this time, but God would still use him to do amazing things.

God was behind the rescue plan and He can do anything!

But I keep messing up and giving in to the same old sin. God won't want to use me in His plans.

Wow!

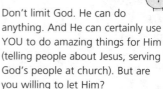

Don't limit God. He can do anything. And He can certainly use YOU to do amazing things for Him (telling people about Jesus, serving God's people at church). But are you willing to let Him?

Pray!

Ask God to use you to serve Him. But watch out, because He will!

6

Prayer under pressure

**Exodus
2 v 23-25**

Family illness.

Depression.

*Natural disasters
like hurricanes
and earthquakes.*

*Events like these
cause awful
suffering.*

Yet it's at times like these that
many people turn to God for help.
Even the most unlikely people **pray**
in a crisis.

Think!

Do you only talk to God in
emergencies and when you want
Him to do stuff? Or do you talk to
Him whatever is happening in your
life?

The Israelites in Egypt had not
been praying to God at all. Perhaps
they'd been praying to Egyptian
idols instead!

Read Exodus 2 v 23-25

*What happened when life got tough
for them? Cross out the **A**s, **M**s and
Ks and follow the maze.*

A	M	K	M	I	E	D	K
M	K	Y	C	R	M	O	A
A	K	E	M	A	K	U	A
→ T	H	M	M	K	T	T	T
A	A	M	K	A	K	M	O
M	K	A	M	K	D	O	G
K	P	L	E	M	F	A	M
M	A	A	H	R	O	A	K

T_ _ _ _ _ _ _ _

_ _ _ _ _ _ _ _

_ _ _ _ _ _ _ _ **(v23)**

It was only when they were
desperate that they started to pray.

What did God remember? (v24)

His c_____

Check out God's covenant with
Abraham in **Genesis 17 v 6-8**.

God promised to be with His people
the Israelites. And He promised
to make them into a great nation
and give them their own land. God
would rescue them from Egypt!

God promises to be with all of His
people. He hears our prayers too!

Pray!

Talk to God now. Think of three
things to THANK Him for.
Then say SORRY to Him for any
times you've disobeyed Him
recently.
Finally, ASK Him to help you with
any problems you have.

WEIRD WORDS

King of Egypt
Pharaoh Thutmose III

Covenant
An agreement God
made with His
people

1

Fire power

The Israelite slaves cried to God for help.

Will God do anything to help them?

And what does Moses have to do with it?

WEIRD WORDS

Midian
Area where Moses was living

Horeb
AKA Mount Sinai, where God would give Moses the 10 Commandments

Holy ground
Moses was near God so must show Him respect

All of today's answers are in the word pool.

> afraid   burn   bush
> Egypt   God   holy   Israelites
> mountain   Pharaoh   rescue
> sandals   seen   sheep   you
> land   Lord   Moses

Read Exodus 3 v 1-6

Moses was looking after his father-in-law's s_____, near God's holy m_____ (v1). The angel of the L_____ appeared to Moses in a flaming b_____ which didn't b_____ up (v2). God called to M_____ (v4) and told him to take off his s_____ because he was standing on h_____ ground (v5). When Moses realised he was speaking to G_____ he was a_____ to look at Him (v6).

Moses was rightly afraid because he knew how puny and sinful he was compared to God.

Think!

Do you show God the respect He deserves? Even if God is your friend, He's also the perfect Creator of the universe! We should remember that when we talk to God.

Read verses 7-10

God said: "I have s_____ my people's misery in E_____ (v7). So I have come down to r_____ them, to take them to a great new l_____ (v8). So I'm sending y_____ (Moses) to P_____ to bring the I_____ out of Egypt (v10).

God would rescue His people from Egypt. And He would use Moses to do it! That must have been a big shock for Moses!

Pray!

Thank God that He cares so much for His people. Ask Him to help you talk to Him respectfully, in the right way.

8

God has promised to rescue the Israelites from Egypt.

And He wants Moses to lead them out.

But is Moses up to the task?

Burning question

Read Exodus 3 v 10-12

Moses didn't think he was the man for the job and started making excuses. *What did God say to him in verse 12?*

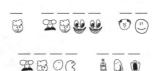

By ourselves we're weak, useless, sinful humans. But God is with His people and can use Christians to do amazing things!

Read verses 13-15
What name did God call Himself?

What would the name I AM mean to Moses and the Israelites?

God is the God of their

God never

He will be their God

Wow!
The God of the Israelites is our God too! He has always existed. He is perfect and will never change. And He will rule His people for ever!

Pray!
Quickly jot down some amazing things you know about God.

_____

_____

_____

_____

Now spend time praising and thanking God for those things.

A B C E F G H I L M N O R S T U V W Y

9

God appeared to Moses in a burning bush and told Moses how He would rescue the Israelites from Egypt.

It's a date

Do you or your family have a calendar? It's probably jammed full of stuff you plan to do.

In today's Exodus bit we can see what God has planned for the Israelites. Not only the events, but the **results** too!

Read Exodus 3 v 16-22

Complete the calendar, using the verses you've just read.

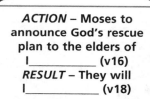

**ACTION – Moses to announce God's rescue plan to the elders of I_____ (v16)
RESULT – They will I_____ (v18)**

**ACTION – Moses to ask the king of E_____ to let the Israelites go into the w_____ to offer God s_____ (v18)
RESULT – The king of Egypt will n____ let them go (v19)**

**ACTION – God to strike the E_____ with terrifying signs and wonders (v20)
RESULT – The king of Egypt would let them g____ (v20)**

**ACTION – God to make the Egyptians show kindness to the Israelites (v21)
RESULT – They will give the Israelites s_____, g_____ and clothes (v22)**

The Israelites were slaves in Egypt and cried out to God for help. God heard their prayers and promised to rescue them in a spectacular way. God told Moses exactly how He would do it (you can read ahead in Exodus to see if it all happened!).

Yesterday we read how God is the great **I AM**: He has always existed, He never changes and will rule for ever. God knows everything that has happened and everything that will happen. So He could tell Moses what would happen to the Israelites.

Wow!

God knows all about you. And He knows what plans He has for you in the future. We don't need horoscopes or fortune-telling! We have a perfect God who is in control of our future!

Pray!

Thank God that your future is safe in His hands. Ask Him to use you to serve Him loads in the future.

**Exodus
4 v 1-9**

*Someone in
your class tells
you that they've
been invited
to have dinner
with the Queen
at Buckingham
Palace.*

*Would you
believe them?*

YES/NO _____

Fire proof

You'd probably think they were messing you around. But if they showed you the official invitation... you would have to believe their **proof**.

Read Exodus 4 v 1

Moses had seen God in the burning bush, but now he had a burning question...

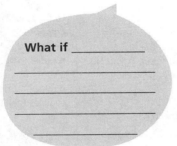

What if _____
_____
_____
_____
_____

Moses wasn't well known to the Israelite leaders, so why should they listen to his wild story?

Read verses 2-9

God gave Moses three signs to show the Israelite leaders, to prove God had appeared to him. *Fill in the missing words and then fit them into the crossword.*

SIGN 1 Moses' (1) __ __ __ __ __ turned into a

(2) __ __ __ __ __

SIGN 2 When he put his

(3) __ __ __ __ into his cloak, it was covered with

(4) __ __ __ __ __ __ __

SIGN 3 If Moses took

(5) __ __ __ __ __ from the river and

(6) __ __ __ __ __ __ it out it would turn to

(7) __ __ __ __ __

God would give Moses these special signs as proof that He would rescue the Israelites.

Think!

God has given us even more proof. He sent His Son JESUS, to rescue us from sin. And He's given us the BIBLE, which tells us all about Jesus and how He died to rescue us. Are you convinced by the proof yet? Have you asked Jesus to rescue you?

WEIRD WORDS

Staff
A shepherd's walking stick

Leprous
All the skin was white and flaky and disgusting

Nile
The world's longest river

Excuse me!

**Exodus
4 v 10-17**

> Sorry, I'm erm... doing something else.

Do you ever make excuses to get out of things?

Action!

What do you try to get out of doing, by making excuses?

_____

_____

tidying my bedroom

_____

_____

Moses had been given the task of standing up to Pharaoh and leading the Israelites' escape from Egypt. No wonder he was making excuses...

Read Exodus 4 v 10-13

Fill in the vowels to reveal Moses' excuse.

> I'm n__t v__ry
> g__ __d at sp__ __k__ng

What was God's reply?

> I w__ll h__lp y__ __
> to sp__ __k

Then Moses' true feelings came out...

> Pl__ __se s__nd
> s__me__ne __lse

Moses couldn't face it. How would God react to being turned down?

Read verses 14-17

1. God was __ngry

Moses was scared and tried to get out of doing what God told him to do. Even Christians can anger God by their unwillingness to obey Him.

2. God was very p__tient

Moses was terrified of speaking to the Israelite leaders and to Pharaoh. So God gave Moses a helper — his brother Aaron. God is patient with us too. He doesn't give up on us when we let Him down. And He gives us far more chances than we deserve.

Think & pray!

How have you disobeyed the Lord recently?

_____

_____

_____

Say sorry to God. Ask Him to help you obey Him more and stop making excuses.

WEIRD WORDS

Eloquent
A good speaker

Mute
Unable to talk

Levite
From the family of Levi, one of Joseph's brothers

Child's play

*Moses finally
stopped making
excuses and set
off to Egypt to
ask Pharaoh
to release the
Israelites.*

WEIRD WORDS

Staff of God
The stick that Moses
used for doing
miracles

Lodging place
A place to stay for
the night

Flint knife
Flint is a sharp rock

**Bridegroom
of blood**
Sorry, I've no idea
what that means!

Read Exodus 4 v 18-23

*What did God tell Moses to do
when he met Pharaoh? (v21)*

*Would Pharaoh listen to Moses and
let the Israelites go? (v21)*

Pharaoh would refuse to obey
God, so God would punish him
by hardening his heart. Pharaoh
wanted to live his own way, not
God's. So God would give him what
he wanted.

*What did God call the Israelites?
(v22)*

Israel is my
_____

The Israelites were God's special
people, His children. They would
be treated brilliantly by God and be
given so much by Him, just as eldest
(firstborn) sons were.

Wow!

Look up John 1 v 12. All
Christians are God's children! They
will often be given a tough time by
people who don't love God (like
Pharaoh). But God looks after them!

Read Exodus 4 v 24-26

Circumcision

God said that all Israelite males
must have a piece of skin around
the penis cut off (Genesis 17 v
12). It was a sign of belonging to
God's family.

Moses had disobeyed God by not
circumcising his son. God was
going to kill Moses, until Moses'
wife (Zipporah) saved the day by
circumcising their son.

Sin is serious. We can't take
obeying God lightly. He hates it
when we disobey Him.

Pray!

Ask God to help you take sin
more seriously, so that you obey
Him more and please Him more.
And thank God that Christians
are His children, who He loves
and cares for.

**Exodus
4 v 27-31**

Ever bumped into a relative or friend you've not seen for ages?

It can be weird seeing how people have changed, and seeing if you still get on with them.

WEIRD WORDS

Mountain of God
Mount Sinai, a special mountain for God and His people. Later, God would give Moses the 10 Commandments there.

Elders
Leaders

Keep your Aaron!

Read Exodus 4 v 27-28

Who did God send to meet Moses?

Moses had been in a foreign country, away from the Israelites, for 40 years! He must have been thrilled to see Aaron again.

Moses told Aaron everything that God had said to him. Earlier Moses had been terrified about going back to Egypt. But now there were two of them to face the Israelites and Pharaoh. A good partnership!

But would the partnership work?

Read verses 29-31

To show what happened, fill in the missing first letters of words.

1. __oses and Aaron __athered all the __sraelite __eaders __ogether

2. __aron __old them __verything __od had __aid

3. They __erformed all the __igns and __iracles God had shown them. Remember what they were? (Exodus 4 v 1-9)

- Moses' __taff turned into a __nake
- His __and was covered with __eprosy
- He poured __ater from the __ile on the __round and it became __lood

4. The __eople __elieved that God had spoken to __oses and had __eard their __rayers

5. The __sraelites __owed down to God and __orshipped Him

All Christians are **God's children**. They are brothers and sisters who serve God together. Who can you get together with to worship God and serve Him together?

Pray!

Do you have a Christian friend? If so, thank God for them and ask Him to show you how to work together for Him.
If not, you could ask God to give you a Christian friend...

The last straw

14

**Exodus
5 v 1-14**

The Israelites were treated cruelly by the Egyptians.

They were slaves, forced to do back-breaking work.

WEIRD WORDS

Labour
Work

Numerous
Loads of them!

Quota
The number of bricks they were expected to make

Stubble
Little bits of straw left after the harvest

Now fill in what's happened so far.

> **God had h_____
> their cry for help. He sent
> M_____ and Aaron to
> visit P_____ and ask
> him to l_____ the
> Israelites go.**

Now fit those words into the grid.

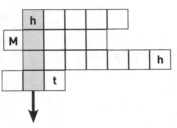

At last there was

for the Israelites!

God's people must have been excited as these two men prepared for their big meeting with Pharaoh. At last they'd be freed from slavery! But it wouldn't be quite so easy...

Read Exodus 5 v 1-5

What did Pharaoh say?

> **I do not k_____
> the L_____ and
> I will not let
> I_____ go**

Read verses 6-14

> **Pharaoh ordered the
> Israelites to make b_____
> but refused to give them
> any s_____ (v7). Yet they
> were still expected to make
> the same number.**

It was impossible to make good bricks without straw. Pharaoh was punishing God's people.

Wow!

Living for God can be really hard sometimes. People might treat you badly because you're a Christian. It can seem hopeless sometimes. But God is with you and He will help you through the tough times.

Pray!

Pray for anyone you know who is given a hard time for being a Christian. Ask God to encourage them and help them to keep going.

If you would like a free fact sheet on *Facing tough times*, email discover@thegoodbook.co.uk or check out www.thegoodbook.co.uk/contact-us to find our UK mailing address.

Blame game

**Exodus
5 v 15-23**

Pharaoh refused to let the Israelites go into the desert to worship God.

And now he's forcing them to do impossible work.

Read Exodus 5 v 15-18

Pharaoh was sinful and ungodly but he was very clever.

By making life impossible for the Israelites, he was turning them against Aaron and Moses.

Read verses 19-21

Go back one letter to reveal what the Israelites said to Moses and Aaron.

Z P V   I B W F

H J W F O

Q I B S B P I

B O   F Y D V T F

U P   L J M M   V T

They no longer believed that Moses would lead them out of Israel and they blamed him for the trouble they were in.

Read verses 22-23

What did Moses say to God?

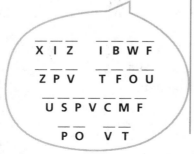

X I Z   I B W F

Z P V   T F O U

U S P V C M F

P O   V T

Moses doubted that God would rescue His people. And he blamed God for the trouble they were in.

Think!

Do you ever blame God for bad stuff that happens?

Don't blame God. He has perfect plans for us for us. Sometimes He lets bad stuff happen to show us what sinners like Pharaoh are really like. And how different God is. So we'll turn from sin and trust Him.

The **great news** is that God has done something about our suffering. He sent Jesus to die in our place so that we can have our sins forgiven. Christians will go to live with God in heaven, where there will be no more sin, suffering or sadness!

Pray!

Ask God to help you to trust Him more. Thank Him that He sent Jesus to put an end to your sadness for ever.

WEIRD WORDS

Overseers
People in charge of the workers

Full quota
The amount of bricks they were expected to make

Obnoxious
Unpleasant and offensive

**Exodus
6 v 1-5**

*Pharaoh is now
treating the
Israelites even
more cruelly.*

*So they're
blaming Moses
and Aaron for
their suffering.*

*And Moses is
blaming God
for the whole
situation.*

WEIRD WORDS

Covenant
Agreement that
God made with the
Israelites

Resided
Lived

Showing promise

> Lord, why have you
> brought trouble on us?
> You've not rescued your
> people at all!

Read Exodus 6 v 1-5

*You can find all the missing words
in the wordsearch.*

R	D	E	C	A	N	A	A	N	B
O	E	H	D	T	F	N	U	V	G
J	P	M	O	J	A	C	O	B	R
C	O	V	E	N	A	N	T	D	O
O	N	Y	E	M	H	Q	F	R	A
U	G	A	B	H	B	K	L	I	N
N	X	S	T	E	S	E	M	V	I
T	L	G	Q	A	Z	K	R	E	N
R	P	H	A	R	A	O	H	E	G
Y	P	R	J	D	M	C	R	S	D

1. God of answers

"I will force P_____ to
d_____ my people out of
his c_____." (v1)

God would rescue His people. But
God doesn't always answer our
prayers immediately.

And He might answer them in a way
we're not expecting. Yet He **does**
hear us and He **will** answer our
prayers. His timing is perfect!

2. God of promise

"I made a c_____
with Abraham, Isaac and
J_____. I promised
to give them the land of
C_____." (v3-4)

God promised His people far more
than they deserved, including giving
them somewhere to live. And God
has promised to give all Christians
somewhere to live — in eternity
with Him!

3. God of compassion

"I have h_____
the g_____ of
the Israelites. I have
r_____ my
covenant." (v5)

God saw His people suffering and
would rescue them. God cares for
us and longs to rescue us from
suffering too.

Pray!

You've got loads to thank God
for! Thank Him that...
1. You can talk to Him and He
   hears your prayers.
2. He always keeps His promises.
3. He cares for you so much!

17

**Exodus
6 v 6-27**

*The Israelites
have turned
against God and
His messenger,
Moses.*

WEIRD WORDS

Yoke
The suffering of
being slaves

Redeem
Buy back, rescue

**Swore with
uplifted hand**
Promised

Faltering lips
Moses wasn't a good
public speaker

Sad habits

*Today's missing words can be found
in the **backwards word pool**.*

netsil   hoarah
desimorp   degaruocsid
dnal   doG   elpoep   sesoM
snaitpygE   yrevals

Read Exodus 6 v 6-8

**God promised to free the
Israelites from s_____
and rescue them from the
E_____ (v6). They
would be God's p_____
and He would be their
G_____ (v7). He would take
them to the l_____ He
had p_____
them (v8).**

What fantastic promises! Surely the
Israelites would be excited...

Read verses 9-12

**M_____ told the Israelites
what God had said but they
wouldn't l_____ to
him because they were
d_____ by
how cruelly P_____
was treating them (v9).**

Sadly, people are sometimes so
upset by bad stuff in their lives
that they stop trusting God. They
don't believe that He will end
their tough times.

Wow!

But God will rescue His people.
When Jesus comes again, all sin will
be dealt with and God's people will
be freed from suffering and sadness
for ever!

Skim read verses 13-27

This list of Moses and Aaron's family
was probably meant to let people
reading it know exactly who Moses
and Aaron were.

They could see that God used these
two normal Israelites to do amazing
things!

Pray!

Do you know anyone who has
stopped trusting God? Maybe
yourself? Ask God to remind
them how loving He is. And that
they can trust Him even when life
seems hard.

*We'll find out what happens next
for the Israelites later in this issue...*

**Acts
14 v 1-7**

The book of Acts is all about how Jesus' followers began to spread the gospel.

The gospel is the good news that Jesus died for our sins and was raised back to life!

WEIRD WORDS

Iconium
Now called Konya, in Turkey

Gentiles
Non-Jews

Apostles
Paul and Barnabas, who'd been sent to tell people about Jesus

Acts: Gospel gets around

Read Acts 13 v 49-52 to see what had happened at the last place Paul and Barnabas had told people about Jesus.

Circle the right option every time you're given a choice.

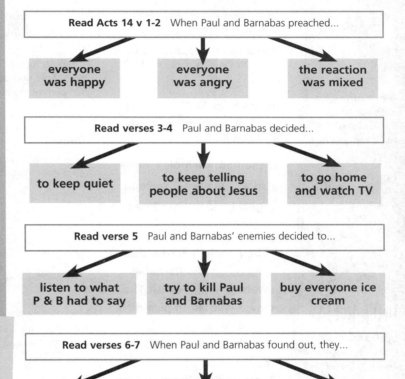

Read Acts 14 v 1-2 When Paul and Barnabas preached...

| everyone was happy | everyone was angry | the reaction was mixed |

Read verses 3-4 Paul and Barnabas decided...

| to keep quiet | to keep telling people about Jesus | to go home and watch TV |

Read verse 5 Paul and Barnabas' enemies decided to...

| listen to what P & B had to say | try to kill Paul and Barnabas | buy everyone ice cream |

Read verses 6-7 When Paul and Barnabas found out, they...

| cried a lot | decided to stay where they were and keep quiet | went somewhere else but kept telling people about Jesus |

Telling people about Jesus will make some people angry. When this happened, Paul and Barnabas sometimes stuck around and sometimes moved on. **But they never stopped telling people about Jesus.**

Pray!

Ask God to help you tell people about Jesus and never give up.

Idle idol worship

**Acts
14 v 8-20**

*We're travelling
with Paul and
Barnabas as they
tell people about
Jesus.*

*Amazing things
are bound to
happen...*

WEIRD WORDS

Lystra
City in the country
now called Turkey

Wreaths
Flowers

Sacrifices
Gifts offered to fake
gods to please them

Testimony
Evidence that He's
the real God

Read Acts 14 v 8-10

Look at the amazing effect the good
news about Jesus had on this man!
He believed that Jesus had died for
him and could heal him too. He'd
been crippled since he was born but
God healed him!

The crowd were amazed, but not in
a way Paul and Barnabas liked…

Read verses 11-18

*Use the words in the **backwards**
word pool to fill in the gaps.*

sabanraB   sehtolc   htrae

sdog   nevaeh   snamuh

gnivil   luaP   secifircas

**The people believed that
P_____ and Barnabas
were g_____ (v11)! The
crowd wanted to give gifts
and offer s_____
to them (v13). Paul and
B_____ were so
upset by this that they tore
their c_____ (v14).**

**Paul said that they were
h_____, not gods
(v15). He told the crowd to
stop worshipping false gods
and turn to the l_____
God, who made h_____
and e_____ (v15).**

We sometimes worship false gods
too. A false god can be **anything**
that becomes more important to us
than God.

Think!

What things do people
make more important than God?

_____

_____

_____

_____

Most of these things are not wrong.
But we shouldn't put them first in
our lives, instead of God.

Read verses 19-20

Paul was almost killed for telling the
truth about God. But it didn't stop
him! Tomorrow, we'll read how he
carried on serving God.

Pray!

Say sorry for the things you put
first instead of God. Ask Him to
help you to worship and serve
Him, nothing else.

**Acts
14 v 21-28**

Share where?

They've had two long years of travelling and telling people about Jesus. Now Barnabas and Paul are finally on their way home.

Read Acts 14 v 21-25

On the map, draw arrows to show Paul and Barnabas' route back home. Start in Derbe (v20).

What did Paul and Barnabas do to make sure God's work carried on after they had left?

They str_____ed the

disciples, en_____ing

them to stick at it (v22).

They encouraged all the Christians to keep going with the task of telling people about Jesus, even when they were given a hard time for it.

WEIRD WORDS

Gospel
The message that Jesus died to rescue people

Disciples
Followers of Jesus

Hardships
Tough times

Kingdom of God
Living with God ruling your life

Elders
Church leaders

Fasting
Going without food to spend extra time talking to God

Gentiles
Non-Jewish people

Action!

Do you know any Christians you could encourage to stick at serving God?

_____

_____

Meet up with them this week to chat and pray. Maybe you could send them an encouraging note or email too!

Read verses 26-28

When they got back home, Paul and Barnabas grabbed the whole church and told them everything God had done for them on their travels!

Think!

Write down some of the things God has done for you.

_____

_____

_____

_____

_____

_____

Now the hard part — grab Christian friends and family and share some of these things with them. Maybe they can also encourage you with stories from their lives too.

Spot the difference

Read Acts 15 v 1-4

A lot of people had turned to Jesus and become Christians. Some of them were from Jewish families and some were not.

*To reveal what some of the Jewish Christians said, **go back one letter** (B=A, C=B, D=C).*

    _ _ _ _ _ _
    V O M F T T

    _ _ _   _ _ _
    Z P V   B S F

    _ _ _ _ _ _ _ _ _ _
    D J S D V N D J T F E

    _ _ _   _ _ _ _ _ _
    Z P V   D B O O P U

    _ _   _ _ _ _ _
    C F   T B W F E

Paul and Barnabas knew that this was untrue. So they set off to Jerusalem to sort it out. They knew that **faith in Jesus** is the only thing that can save people from their sin.

But they didn't argue on everything. Look at verses 3-4. **All** the Christians thought it was great that Gentiles were turning away from their sins and turning to Jesus!

Think!
Are YOU excited when you hear about people becoming Christians?

Read verses 5-11

Let's see how **God** compares Jews and Gentiles.

Jews
Who did God give to help the Jewish Christians (v8)?
H_____ **S**_____
How were they saved (v11)?
By J_____ **C**_____

Gentiles
Who did God give to help the Gentile Christians (v8)?
H_____ **S**_____
How were they saved (v11)?
By J_____ **C**_____

To God, there was **no difference** between Jews and Gentiles! When Jesus died on the cross, He died so that **anyone** could be put right with God.

Wow!

If we put our faith in Jesus then He'll save us from our sins. It doesn't matter what our background is. Or if we've been circumcised or not.

Pray!

Know any Christians who are hard to love? Jesus loves them enough that He died to save them! Ask God to help you love them too.

God's got the answers

**Acts
15 v 12-21**

Lots of Jesus' followers have gathered together in Jerusalem.

They're trying to decide if Gentiles (non-Jews) who become Christians have to be circumcised. Should the Gentiles have to follow all the old Jewish rules? It's a tricky one...

Read Acts 15 v 12-18

*Where did James find the answer? Cross out all the **X**s, **Y**s and **Z**s to find out.*

```
YXHXZEFOXUYZZXNYDT
XYZYHEYXAZNSYYZXWE
ZYYXZRYYINXXGZXYZOD
SXYZYXWYYZXOXRYZZXD

H_____

_____

_____
```

James found the answer in God's Word – the Bible. James knew the Old Testament really well.

He remembered that Amos the prophet said that some Gentiles would be part of God's people.

Wow!

Unsure about something? Going through a tough time? The first place to look is the Bible. If you're not sure where to look in the Bible, ask an older Christian. Or email us:
discover@thegoodbook.co.uk

WEIRD WORDS

Assembly
Everyone there

James
Jesus' brother

Prophets
Men who told God's people what God wanted to say to them

Abstain
Don't do it!

Idols
False gods

Immorality
Sin

Synagogues
Where Jewish people met to learn from God's Word

Sabbath
Saturday

Read verses 19-21

James was saying...

We shouldn't make it harder for people to become Christians (v19). So we should not expect Gentiles to get circumcised. But they should try not to do things that offend us Jewish Christians (v20).

Think!

Is there anything you do that could have a bad effect on other Christians around you? Maybe they find it unhelpful that you watch or read certain things...

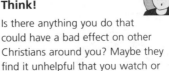

Pray!

Ask God to help you encourage other people to live God's way rather than make it difficult for them. And ask God to teach you loads from the Bible to help you!

23

Acts 15 v 22-35

WEIRD WORDS

Apostles
People sent out to tell others about Jesus

Elders
Church leaders

Authorisation
Agreement

Holy Spirit
The Helper that God has given to all Christians

Burden you
Weigh you down

Abstain
Don't do it!

Prophets
Men who told people what God wanted to say to them

Believers
Christians

Get scribbling!

Read Acts 15 v 22-29

The Christians in Jerusalem wrote a letter to Gentiles who had become Christians. It mentioned the decision we read about yesterday. They also wanted to **encourage** these Christians.

Read verses 30-35

There were two main ways they encouraged these Christians.

1. Writing to them

It encouraged these Christians to know that the guys in Jerusalem were remembering them and praying for them.

It's nice to get letters and emails. We can encourage other Christians (especially ones in difficult or lonely situations) by writing to them.

Action!

Who will you encourage with a letter or an email?

_____

_____

_____

_____

2. Speaking to them

We spend a lot of time talking (some of us more than others!). But how well do you use that time? _Fill in the chart below. Estimate how much time you spend each day talking about these different subjects._

Subject	Hours	Mins
TV/Films		
Music		
Friends		
Clothes		
Sport		
School		
Jesus		

Pray!

Thank God for the people who have encouraged you. Ask God to give them someone to encourage them too. Maybe you? Ask Him to show YOU how you could encourage Christians you know.

Now get encouraging people! Write those letters and emails!

It's sad when people fall out with each other.

Even the most mature Christians do it sometimes.

Even Paul and Barnabas fell out.

WEIRD WORDS

Believers
Christians

Barnabash

Read Acts 15 v 36-41

Paul and Barnabas had been through so much together:

- threats from Jewish leaders
- attacked by crowds
- disagreement in the church
- God used them to do amazing things
- many people became followers of Jesus

Now it was all over because of an argument. But God hadn't finished using Paul and Barnabas yet...

Read verses 39-40 again
and fill in the missing numbers.

Before

_____ pair of missionaries

_____ place that would hear about Jesus

After

_____ pairs of missionaries

_____ places that would hear about Jesus

Even when we spoil the good things God does, He can still turn things around and make good come out of it!

I wonder if Paul and Barnabas regretted their argument. Read what Paul wrote some time later in **Ephesians 4 v 26**.

Paul warns us not to let anger lead us to do or say things we shouldn't. And when we do lose our cool, we should sort things out quickly rather than letting them get worse.

Think!

Have you fallen out with anyone recently?

What can you do to make things right between you?

Do something to put things right in the next **24 hours**.

Pray!

Ask God to help you not spoil your friendships with arguments. If you do mess up, ask God to help you say sorry and put things right.

Have you emailed or written to the people you wrote down yesterday?

**Acts
16 v 1-10**

Timothy

*Paul and
Barnabas had
an argument
and went their
separate ways.*

*So Paul took Silas
with him to tell
more and more
people about
Jesus.*

WEIRD WORDS

Greek
He spoke Greek and
wasn't a Jew

Province
Large area of land,
like a country

Macedonia
Find it in an atlas!

Tim fits in

Read Acts 16 v 1-5

*The towns mentioned in these
verses can be found on the map on
day 20.*

*Who did Paul and Silas meet in
Lystra (v1)?*

T_____

Jewish boys were usually circumcised
(a piece of skin around the penis
cut off) when they were 8 days old.
But although Timothy's mum was
Jewish, his dad wasn't, and Timothy
hadn't been circumcised.

Remember the argument about
circumcision? (See day 21 if you
don't!) Some people thought you
had to be circumcised to be a
Christian. Paul knew that was not
true. But he circumcised Timothy
so that other Jews might accept
Timothy and listen to what he told
them about Jesus!

And people did listen to them! Verse
5 tells us that more people became
Christians every day!

Read verses 6-10

On the map on this page, find
where Paul and co went next.

*Where did God's Holy Spirit tell
them not to go (v6-7)?*

Go back one letter to find out.

_ _ _ _
B T J B

_ _ _ _ _ _ _ _
C J U I Z O J B

*In a vision, where did God tell Paul
to go (v9)?*

_ _ _ _ _ _ _ _ _
N B D F E P O J B

Wow!

God shows Christians
what He wants them to do. But He
doesn't use dreams all the time!
We're more likely to find out what
God wants us to do by reading His
Word, the Bible. And by asking Him
when we pray.

Pray!

If you mean it, ask God to show
you how you can best serve Him.

Purple heart

Acts
16 v 11-15

In a dream, God told Paul (and Silas and Timothy) to go to Macedonia and preach about Jesus there.

WEIRD WORDS

Roman colony
Place ruled by the Romans

Sabbath
Saturday, Jewish holy day

Household
Family

Baptised
Being dunked in water to show that God has washed away your wrongs

Read Acts 16 v 11-12

Did you notice the "we" in verse 11? This shows that Luke, the writer of Acts, was with them on this trip too!

Cross out the wrong words to reveal what Luke tells us.

We left Troas/Texas and sailed/soiled to Samaria/Samothrace and then on to Neath/New York/Neapolis. From there we travelled to Philippi/Philip's house in Manchester/Macedonia, a place run by the Greeks/Romans/Welsh. We stayed there a few days/weeks.

Read verses 13-15

and reveal what happened next.

On the Sabbath/Sunday we went to the city gate/river to find a place to chat/pray/play baseball.

We spoke to the women/men gathered there. One of them was Lucy/Lydia who sold pink/puce/purple cloth.

The Lord opened her heart/mind/cloth to what Paul was saying. She became a believer and was bashed/baptised. She then invited Paul and the others to stay in her house/hotel/purple cloth.

LYDIA'S PURPLE EMPORIUM

Lydia had become a believer. She persuaded Paul and the others to stay at her house. Isn't that great? As soon as she became a believer, Lydia wanted to help Paul.

Action

How can you help Christians who tell people about Jesus? Send encouraging letters and emails? Help them with a kids' club at church?

_____

_____

_____

_____

Pray!

Think carefully about what you want to do to help other Christians. Now ask God to help you actually do it!

John
1 v 1-5

We're now going to start reading the book of John.

In it, the disciple John tells the story of Jesus' life.

Check out John 20 v 31 to find out why he wrote it.

Go on, look it up right now!

Pretty good reason, eh?

John: Word on the street

Read John 1 v 1-2

Who is John writing about?

The W_____

Who does John mean? Cross out the letters W O R D to find out.

> **W J O R D E W O S**
> **R D W U O R S D**

J_____

He's talking about Jesus!

Read verses 1 and 2 out loud. This time, replace *"the Word"* with *"Jesus"*.

We're already learning some amazing facts about Jesus...

Fact 1
Jesus is God (v1)

The whole book of John is all about this amazing fact!

Fact 2
Jesus has always been around and always will be (v2)

What else can we learn about Jesus?

Read verses 3-5

Fact 3
Jesus created the world, the universe, everything! (v3)

Fact 4
Jesus brings life and light to the world (v4)

Trusting in Jesus is the only way to everlasting life with God. He's the only one we should follow.

Fact 5
Sin and death (darkness) cannot defeat Jesus! (v5)

By dying on the cross and being raised back to life, Jesus beat sin and death!

Pray!

Take time now to go through each of the 5 facts about Jesus. Thank and praise Jesus for each one.

28 DeLIGHTful news

John
1 v 5-13

John is telling us about Jesus coming into the world.

Jesus is the LIGHT who shows us the truth about ourselves and the truth about God.

Write down what life would be like without light...

We wouldn't be able to see. Everyone would be blind.

But without Jesus in their lives, people are blind. We need Him in order to see the way things really are.

Read John 1 v 5-9

God even sent a man called John the Baptist to tell people about Jesus. (Not the same John who's telling the story!) John the Baptist told people that Jesus was the light they needed in their lives.

But what was their reaction?

WEIRD WORDS

The light
Jesus Christ

Testify
Tell people about Jesus

Natural descent
Human parents

Read verses 10-11

Th__y d__d n__t
r__c__ __v__ H__m

Tragedy! God sent His Son Jesus into the world as a way of ending their ignorance (blindness) about Him. But people wouldn't accept Jesus!

Yet what happens to people who do accept Jesus?

Read verses 12

Th__y b__c__m__
ch__ldr__n __f G__d!

Wow!

That offer is for everyone who receives Jesus, believes Him and lives for Him!

They become God's children. God is their Father who will love and care for them forever!

Think!

Have you accepted Jesus?
Are you one of God's children?

For free info on *how to become one of God's children (a Christian),* email discover@thegoodbook.co.uk or check out www.thegoodbook.co.uk/contact-us to find our UK mailing address.

What's God like?

29

**John
1 v 14-18**

*Time to learn
loads more
about Jesus.*

*Use the words
down the centre
of the page to
fill in today's
gaps.*

WEIRD WORDS

The Word
Jesus Christ

Flesh
Human

Dwelling
Home

Grace
Giving people far
more than they
deserve

Surpassed me
Is far greater than
me

Read John 1 v 14

That all sounds a bit confusing!
So here's what John is telling us
about Jesus.

**1. Jesus came down
from heaven, became a
h_____ and
l_____ among people**

Jesus is God, yet He came and lived
on earth!

**2. Jesus was the one and
o_____ Son**

God's only Son. There is no one
else like Him!

**3. The people saw His
g_____**

They saw the amazing, miraculous
things Jesus did. Things only God
could do.

**4. Jesus was full of
g_____ and t_____**

He showed great love for people
and did far more for them (and us!)
than they deserved. And He showed
people the truth about God.

Read verses 15-18

These verses are saying the same
things about Jesus as verse 14.

grace only glory herring God truth human being lived

John the Baptist

So read through the four points
you just filled in to remind yourself
of what John's saying.

Worked out what the **BIG**
message is yet?

Jesus is G_____!

Want to know what God is like?
Then look at Jesus!

Action!

On scrap paper, write a list of words
that describe Jesus.

That's what God is like!

Pray!

Spend five minutes praising and
thanking God for what He's like.
Use the four facts in bold (and the
list you've made) to help you out.

**John
1 v 19-28**

Who are you?

Read John 1 v 19-23

The priests were saying...

> **What right have you got to go around preaching and baptising?**

So what did John say?

> **I'm not the**
> _____ (v20)

He wasn't the perfect King who God had promised would rescue His people. That was **Jesus!**

> **I'm not E_____ (v21)**

And John wasn't the Old Testament prophet Elijah, come back to earth!

> **I'm not the**
> **P_____ (v21)**

And he wasn't the prophet mentioned in Deuteronomy 18 v 15!

> **I'm the v_____ (v23)**

In other words, it didn't matter who he was, he was just a messenger. God's messenger.

So what was John's message?

Read verses 24-28

WHO DO YOU THINK YOU ARE?

That's a scary question to be asked.

It's one that people were asking John the Baptist.

WEIRD WORDS

Testimony
What he said

Levites
Men who served God in the temple

Pharisees
Very strict Jews

Baptise
See Discover tomorrow!

John doesn't say much about himself because he's telling them about **Jesus!**

It's easy to want people to notice us and be impressed. Especially if we're involved in Christian work. But we should want people to notice **Jesus** and to find out more about Him.

Action!

How can you be more humble, so that people notice Jesus more than they notice you?

_____

_____

_____

_____

_____

Pray!

Ask God to help you to be more humble and to point people towards Jesus instead.

Very important person

John
1 v 29-34

A 😐
B 😊
D ☆
E 😊
F :)
G 😵
H ☾
I 😺
L 😁
M 🔋
N 👁
O 👁
P 😣
R 🐾
S ○
T ○
Y 🍾

John the Baptist is telling everyone about Jesus.

Use the code to decipher what John said about Jesus.

Read John 1 v 29

Jesus is the

In Bible times, a lamb was killed and offered to God as a sacrifice (gift). But Jesus would be the ultimate sacrifice. He would die on the cross to take away the sin of the world!

That means that everyone who trusts in Jesus to forgive them for the wrong stuff they've done will have their sins wiped out! For ever!

Read verses 30-33

Jesus _ _ _ _ _ _ _ _

with the

_ _ _ _ _ _ _ _ _

John baptised people with water. That means he dunked people in water to show that they had turned away from their sinful ways.

But Jesus would baptise people with the **Holy Spirit**. This means that when He went back to heaven, He would send His Spirit to live in the lives of all believers.

Holy Spirit

The Holy Spirit is God. Every Christian has the Holy Spirit with them all the time, helping them live for God!

Read verse 34

Jesus is the

_ _ _ _ _ _ _ _ _

Jesus is **God's Son**. (That's what "God's Chosen One" means.) No one is more important than Jesus! Do you give Jesus the respect He deserves?

Pray!

Thank Jesus that...
1. He gave His life so that you could be forgiven!
2. He has given Christians His Holy Spirit to help them live His way!
3. He is God's Son — far more powerful than anyone else!

WEIRD WORDS

Surpassed me
Is far greater than me

**John
1 v 35-51**

WEIRD WORDS

Disciples
Followers

**Messiah/Christ/
King of Israel**
The perfect King
who God promised
would rescue His
people

The Law
First five books of
the Bible, written
by Moses

The prophets
Men who gave
God's message to
His people

**Ascending and
descending**
Moving up and
down from heaven

Spread it!

Read John 1 v 35-42

Andrew realised that Jesus was the **Messiah** who had come to rescue people. *So what did Andrew do immediately (v41)?*

[blank box]

He told his brother about Jesus.

Action!

Do you know Jesus?
If He's King of your life, who will you tell about Him?

_____

_____

_____

Read verses 43-46

When Philip met Jesus, he did the same thing as Andrew. He rushed off to tell someone about Jesus. To tell him that Jesus is the King, who God promised would rescue His people!

Action!

So how will you tell your friends about Jesus?

_____

_____

_____

Read verses 47-51

Jesus knew all about Nathaniel. And He knows everything about each of us!

Jesus also told Nathaniel that he would see Jesus do amazing things. More about that in the rest of John's book!

Pray!

Ask God to make you more enthusiastic about Jesus. Ask Him to help you tell people about Jesus.

33

**John
2 v 1-12**

In 1999, John Evans balanced a car (a Mini weighing 160kg) on his head for 33 seconds! Amazing!

WEIRD WORDS

Ceremonial washing
Washing to be pure and acceptable to God

Choice wine
The best wine

Glory
His greatness, what He's really like

Faith
Belief, trust

Sign of the wines

We're going to read about Jesus doing something amazing. But it's not just impressive, it tells us something about who Jesus is...

Read John 2 v 1-4

Running out of wine at a wedding was **really embarrassing**. That's why Mary (Jesus' mum) asked Jesus to do something about it. Jesus did it, but He let Mary know that He was on earth to do much more important things!

Read verses 5-10

*What did Mary tell the servants? Find out by taking every **second letter**, starting with the **D** at the top.*

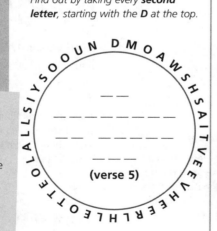

(verse 5)

Think!

That's a good piece of advice for us to remember as we learn more from Jesus in John's book about Him.

Read verse 11-12

This miracle was a **sign** pointing to Jesus' glory – how great He is! The disciples saw it and believed in Jesus and trusted Him. Even though they didn't understand everything about Him.

Pray!

Do you believe and trust in Jesus? Do you live His way?

If so, will you praise Him for how great He is?

If not, will you ask Him to help you trust Him more?

**John
2 v 13-25**

Yesterday, Jesus did something amazing.

Today, Jesus gets angry...

Temple temper?

Read John 2 v 13-17

The temple was the place where **God** was present in a special way. Not a place for selling animals and making money in dishonest ways!

That's why Jesus was so angry.

Look at **verse 17**. It's a quote from Psalm 19, saying how Jesus was devoted to His Father God and to His Father's house (the temple). These people were treating God's house as a money-making shop!

Wow!

It's not always wrong to get angry. Especially when we see people mocking God.

The people wanted to see a miracle to prove that Jesus was God's Son...

Read verses 18-22
What did He say would happen?

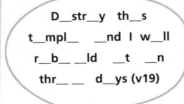

D__str__y th__s t__mpl__ __nd I w__ll r__b__ __ld __t __n thr__ __ d__ys (v19)

Wow!

But Jesus wasn't talking about the temple they were standing in. He was talking about a far more amazing miracle.

Jesus would die a painful death. And then be raised back to life after three days!

Read verses 23-25

Jesus did some miraculous things in Jerusalem. But He could see that the people didn't really have faith in Him. Jesus isn't fooled by outward appearances. He knows exactly what everyone is really like.

Think & pray!

What about you? Do you have faith in Jesus? Do you believe He died and was raised back to life? Spend time talking to God about your answers.

**John
3 v 1-12**

Ever met anyone famous?

The important Pharisee Nicodemus was quite famous.

But he was about to meet someone far more amazing...

Born free

Read John 3 v 1-2

Nicodemus knew Jesus was special, but didn't yet believe that Jesus was **God's Son**.

Read verses 3-7

What did Jesus say that shook Nicodemus' world? Go back one letter to find out (B=A, C=B etc).

— — — — —
O P   P O F

— — — — — — — — —
D B O   T F F   U I F

— — — — — — — — — —
L J O H E P N   P G

— — — — — — — —
H P E   V O M F T T

— — — — — — —
U I F Z   B S F

— — — — — — — — —
C P S O   B H B J O

(v3)

Nicodemus probably thought he was a good, godly man. But Jesus told him he needed to start again. He needed to turn away from his sinful way of living and start living for God. He needed the Holy Spirit (v5-6) to change him and help him to please God.

Having your life completely changed by God is the only way to be a part of God's kingdom (v6).

Read verse 8

We can't see the wind, but we can see its devastating effect on a windy day. And though we can't see the **Holy Spirit**, we can see His huge effect on people's lives.

Read verses 9-12

Nicodemus may have been super-religious, but he'd still not worked out that he needed to have his sin sorted out.

Pray!

Have you been born again? Have you turned your back on sin and started living for God? Spend 5 minutes talking to God about your answer.

Jesus is telling Nicodemus that he needs to be born again and start living for God.

WEIRD WORDS

Son of Man
Jesus

Eternal
Everlasting

Perish
Die and go to hell

Condemn
Punish

Exposed
Revealed

READ THESE VERSES!!!

Read John 3 v 13-15

Wow! Jesus is God's Son.

He came down from heaven to save us from our sins. Soon He would go back to heaven to be with His Father.

What did Moses lift up?

(v14)

In the Old Testament, Moses made a bronze snake. God said that anyone who looked at it would be cured from the deadly snakebites they'd received. (Numbers 21 v 9)

Who else would be lifted up?

(v14)

Anyone who turns to Jesus won't be saved from a snakebite! They will have eternal life with Jesus!

Read verses 16-17

Fill in the gaps please!

God so _____ the world that He gave His one and only _____, so that _____ believes in Him shall not _____ but have eternal _____.

Read through that again, it's amazing! Write out v16 on a sheet of paper and learn it by heart. This is the most amazing truth you'll ever know!!!

It tells us how much God loves us. And how we can be saved from our sinful ways.

But read verses 18-21

Jesus is the Light. Everyone who trusts in Him to forgive them will be rescued from their sins!

But anyone who ignores Jesus and continues to live for themselves will not receive eternal life.

Think!

Have you chosen to live for God in the light? Or to live for yourself in the darkness?

Why did Jesus come?
For a free e-booklet, email
discover@thegoodbook.co.uk
or check out
www.thegoodbook.co.uk/contact-us
to find our UK mailing address.

John the Baptist
has been telling
people about
Jesus. But
now Jesus has
arrived and is
getting all the
attention.

WEIRD WORDS

Ceremonial washing
Washing to be pure
and acceptable to
God

Certified
Proved

The Spirit
The Holy Spirit helps
Christians serve God

Wrath
Punishment

Jealous or joyful?

Read John 3 v 22-26

Many people came to Jesus to be baptised. They were dunked under water as a sign that they had turned away from their old sinful ways. But more people were going to Jesus to be baptised than to John. So did John get jealous?

Read verses 27-35

John wasn't jealous at all! John made a comparison between himself and Jesus to show who people should really be listening to.

From each pair of descriptions, work out which one belongs to John, and which to Jesus. Draw arrows to the right person.

Sent before the Messiah
The Messiah Himself! (v28)
Bridegroom (v29)
Bridegroom's friend
Must become greater
Must become less (v30)
Comes from earth (v31)
Came from heaven
God's Son (v35)
God's servant

John the Baptist　　　**Jesus the Messiah**

John says that Jesus is like a bridegroom — the most important man at a wedding. His followers (the bride) belong to Him. John is the bridegroom's friend who helps the bridegroom. John isn't jealous at all. In fact he's very happy to serve Jesus, God's Son!

Think & pray!

Are you happy to point people to Jesus, as John the Baptist did? Ask God to give you the joy and ability to talk to your friends about Jesus.

Think again!

Read verse 36. Have you made that choice yet? Do you accept Jesus and live for Him? Or do you reject Him and face God's punishment?

38

**John
4 v 1-14**

*The Pharisees
were annoyed
that Jesus had
become very
popular.*

*So Jesus left
the area before
anything bad
happened.*

WEIRD WORDS

Pharisees
Very strict Jews

Baptising
Dunking people in
water as a sign that
they had turned
from sin

Disciples
Followers

Sixth hour
Midday

Eternal life
Living for ever with
Jesus

Thirst things first

Read John 4 v 1-6

On His travels, Jesus had to pass
through Samaria. Jewish people
hated Samaritans and refused to
have anything to do with them. So
would Jesus treat Samaritans in the
same way?

Read verses 7-9

Jewish men wouldn't normally talk
to a Samaritan. And especially not a
Samaritan woman!

Did Jesus ignore this woman?

YES/NO _____

Wow!

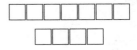

It doesn't matter who
you are. It doesn't matter how
unpopular you are. It doesn't matter
where you're from or what you look
like. Jesus will never turn you away!
He longs to have you as His friend!

Read verses 10-14

Jesus talked about **living water**.
The woman couldn't understand
what living water meant at all. She
wondered how Jesus could give her
water from a deep well when He
didn't even have a bucket!

But Jesus didn't mean that kind of
water. So what did He mean by
living water?

*To find out, fill in the missing letters.
Then stick them in the boxes below
in the same order.*

1. J__sus gives the wa__er
2. It qu__nches thi__st
3. It __ever runs out
   at __ll
4. It's __ike a __iving
   water spring __nside
   of you
5. It gives everlasting
   li__ __

Wow!

What an offer! Eternal life in us,
welling up inside like a bubbling
spring! Will you take Jesus up on
His offer of eternal life?
If you're a Christian, then you
already have!

39

John 4 v 15-26

Jesus is talking about living water.

He means eternal life but the woman still thinks Jesus is talking about water for her to drink.

WEIRD WORDS

Prophet
God's messenger

Salvation
Rescue from sin

Messiah
The perfect King who God promised would come and rescue His people

Salvation solution

Read John 4 v 15-18

Jesus pointed out that she was living a sinful life. That's why she needed **salvation** — to be rescued from her sinful way of life.

She would have to **admit** that she was living a sinful life, before she could be rescued from her wrong ways.

Action!

Below, write a list of some of the wrong things you've done that need putting right.

Be honest.

_____

_____

_____

_____

Are you concerned enough about them to ask Jesus to put them right? He can!

Read verses 19-20

The woman thought Jesus was just a Jewish prophet. She also thought that God had to be worshipped in a specific place.

Read verses 21-26

That sounds confusing, but here's what Jesus is saying.

> Soon, people will be able to worship God **anywhere**, not just in the temple. Samaritans ignore a lot of the Old Testament, which teaches about the **Messiah** who will make this possible.
> **I am this Messiah!**

> God must be worshipped in sp__r__t and in tr__th (v24).

What does that mean???

When we accept Jesus (the truth) into our lives, He gives us His Spirit to help us worship Him in the way we live our lives. Worshipping isn't just singing songs — it's serving God.

Pray!

Ask God to help you worship Him with your whole life, to have Jesus at the centre of it, and to live for Him.

Jabbering about Jesus

John
4 v 27-42

Jesus told the Samaritan woman that He is the Christ.

That's the King the people had been waiting 100s of years for! Wow!

How will she react?

WEIRD WORDS

Testimony
What she had said

Saviour
Rescuer

First, an interruption…

Read John 4 v 27

Jesus' disciples were shocked because religious leaders rarely spoke with women. But Jesus was prepared to do the unexpected to help her.

Think!

Are you prepared to go out of your way to talk to people you normally wouldn't? You might even be able to talk to them about Jesus! List some people you could try talking to...

_____

_____

_____

_____

Read verses 28-30

Fill in the first letter of each word to find out what the woman did.

__OOK __VERYONE __N

__HE __OWN

__O __EE __ESUS

She couldn't keep quiet about Jesus! Do **you** ever get that excited about Jesus?

Read verses 39-42

Many people went to see Jesus. They believed that they needed Him to change their lives!

What did they say?

__ESUS __EALLY __S

__HE __AVIOUR

__F __HE __ORLD

These Samaritans were hated by many people. Yet they realised that Jesus loved them and could save them from their sinful ways.

Wow!

It doesn't matter who you are or where you're from. Jesus can rescue anyone from their sinful lives!

Pray!

Look at the list you wrote earlier. Ask God to help you tell these people about Jesus. Go on, give it a try!

More from John's book about Jesus later on in this issue...

44

Now we zoom all the way back to Exodus, to see how Moses and the Israelites are doing...

WEIRD WORDS

Faltering lips
Moses wasn't a very good speaker

Prophet
God's messenger (Aaron spoke to Pharaoh for God and for Moses)

Mighty acts of judgment
Punishing the Egyptians

Divisions
Loads of Israelites

Exodus: God's rescue plan

The story so far...

God's people (Israelites) were suffering as slaves in Egypt. They cried out to God to rescue them. The Lord chose **Moses** to lead them out of Egypt. But it wouldn't be easy...

Read Exodus 6 v 28-30

Fill in the missing words from the centre of the page.

God told M_____ to go to P_____ and ask him to let the Israelites go. But Moses said: *"Why would Pharaoh l_____ to me?"*

Read Exodus 7 v 1-7

Moses' brother, A_____, would be like a p_____ — God's messenger (v1). He would s_____ for Moses and ask Pharaoh to let the I_____ leave the country (v2).

God would do many m_____ things in E_____ (v3). But Pharaoh would still r_____ to let them go.

Centre word list:
Aaron
Moses
commanded
Pharaoh
prophet
Egypt
punish
83
refuse
Israelites
rescue
listen
speak
Lord
miraculous

So God would p_____ the Egyptians and r_____ the Israelites!

Moses and Aaron did everything the L_____ had c_____ them, even though they were 80 and _____ years old!

God told Moses and Aaron to talk to Pharaoh, even though they knew that Pharaoh wouldn't listen to them. Sometimes, telling people about God can be hard like that. They refuse to listen to us. But God wants us to keep talking to them about Him!

Pray!

Who do you find hard to talk to about God?

_____

_____

Ask God to help you keep telling them about Him, and not give up.

Snake trick

42

Exodus 7 v 8-13

God sent Moses and Aaron to talk to Pharaoh.

Let's see what happened...

Read Exodus 7 v 8-9

and cross out the wrong words.

The Lord said to Maureen/Moses and Aaron: *"When Pharaoh/Fairy tells you to perform your miracle, throw down your stuff/staff/stick and it will become a snake."*

God made it possible for Aaron to do this amazing miracle. It was a sign to Pharaoh that they had been sent by God. And it was also a sign of God's great power.

Read verses 10-13

Elvis/Aaron/Presley threw down his staff in front of Pharaoh, and it became a steak/snake/cake. Pharaoh called up his wise men and magicians/electricians.

They also turned their staffs into snakes. But Aaron's staff followed/swallowed up their staffs! Yet Pharaoh still wouldn't stop/look/listen to them at all.

For a moment, it looked as if these magicians were as powerful as God. But then Aaron's staff swallowed up theirs!

GOD IS FAR MORE POWERFUL THAN ANYONE ELSE!

Now fill in the rest of verse 13...

Pharaoh's heart became hard and he would not listen to them, just _____

_____

_____

God had already told Moses exactly what would happen.

He said that Moses and Aaron would do amazing miracles but Pharaoh wouldn't listen. It was all happening **just as God had said it would.**

Pray!

Thank God that what He says always comes true. We can always trust God.

WEIRD WORDS

Pharaoh
King of Egypt

Staff
Like a walking stick

Sorcerers
Magicians

Secret arts
We don't know if this means just magic tricks, or something more evil from the devil.

43

Blood flood

**Exodus
7 v 14-25**

*God sent Moses
and Aaron to
ask Pharaoh to
let the Israelites
leave Egypt.*

*But Pharaoh
wouldn't listen
and refused to
let God's people
go.*

WEIRD WORDS

Unyielding
Pharaoh wouldn't
change his mind

The Nile
Biggest river in Egypt
(and longest in the
whole world!)

Hebrews
God's special people,
the Israelites

Pharaoh had been warned

↓ ↓

| by a message from God | and by a sign showing God's power |

↓ ↓

But Pharaoh ignored God's warnings

↓

**We've been warned too!
God warns us that anyone
who refuses to turn away
from sin and live His way
will be punished**

↓ ↓

| We're warned by God's words to us in the Bible | And by the greatest sign of all, Jesus dying and coming back to life |

↓ ↓

Don't ignore God's warnings!

Read Exodus 7 v 14-25

*Now in your own words, or pictures,
write or draw what happened.*

*Draw or write stuff in these boxes.
Go on... do it!*

That's all pretty disgusting!

It was a sign that **God was in
charge**, not Pharaoh. But Pharaoh
ignored God, and refused to let the
Israelites go.

Think & pray!

Do you ever ignore God's
warnings in the Bible?
YES/NO _____
Do you think about changing
your ways and then can't be
bothered?
YES/NO _____

Ask God to help you listen to
His warnings, so that you start
living His way and not your
own selfish way.

44

**Exodus
8 v 1-15**

Pharaoh refused to let the Israelites go and worship God, so God turned the Egyptians' water into blood. Yuck!

It's now a week later and Pharaoh still won't let the Israelites go...

WEIRD WORDS

Kneading troughs
Bowls used for making bread

Sacrifices
Gifts to God

Hardened his heart
Refused to obey God

Hop it!

Do you like frogs?

YES/NO _____

You probably won't like them much after this story...

Read Exodus 8 v 1-15

Number the story blocks 1-8 to show the order in which things happened.

(1) God sent Moses to ask Pharaoh to let God's people go.

( ) Moses prayed to God, and God caused the frogs to die.

( ) But Pharaoh's magicians made the same things happen.

( ) God warned Pharaoh that if he refused, God would send thousands of frogs!

( ) But Pharaoh changed his mind and wouldn't let them go.

( ) Pharaoh asked Moses to pray to God to kill the frogs.

( ) Aaron stretched out his staff and thousands of frogs covered the land.

( ) Pharaoh promised to let them go if the frogs went.

Pharaoh desperately asked Moses to get rid of the frogs. *What did Pharaoh promise to do? (v8)*

_____

_____

But did he do it when God got rid of the frogs?

YES/NO _____

People often do what Pharaoh did. In the middle of a crisis they turn to God and ask Him to help them. They might even make promises to Him. But when the problem is solved and life gets back to normal, they forget about God again.

Pray!

We shouldn't just turn to God when life seems tough, then go back to our sinful ways. Ask God to help you talk to Him more often, and to live His way, whether life is tough or terrific.

Itchy and scratchy

45

**Exodus
8 v 16-19**

*Ever been on
holiday, having a
nice time when...*

*the gnats or
mosquitoes
attack!*

*Swarms of tiny
flies biting you
until you itch all
over!*

WEIRD WORDS

Finger of God
God caused the
plague of gnats.
The magicians were
admitting that God
was more powerful
than them.

Read Exodus 8 v 16-17

Pharaoh still refused to let God's
people go into the desert to worship
God. So the Lord sent a plague of
gnats that covered all the people
and animals in Egypt. It must
have been awful. And all because
Pharaoh disobeyed God.

*In the boxes below, look up the
verses and describe the miracles
which God enabled Aaron to do.*

1. Exodus 7 v 9-11

Miracle: _____

_____

_____

**Could Pharaoh's magicians
do the same things?** _____

2. Exodus 7 v 20-22

Miracle: _____

_____

_____

Could the magicians do it?

_____

3. Exodus 8 v 6-7

Miracle: _____

_____

_____

Could the magicians do it?

_____

Read Exodus 8 v 18-19

Wow!

God was far more
powerful than these magicians!
Sometimes it seems as though God
isn't that powerful. Or we forget
that He is in charge. But He is far,
far more powerful than anyone or
anything!

Even the magicians realised that
God was punishing the Egyptians
for disobeying Him. But Pharaoh still
refused to let God's people go.

Think & pray!

Some people refuse to believe in
God and obey Him, despite seeing
evidence of His great power.
Do you know anyone like that?

_____

_____

Ask God to help that person
realise that God is in charge, so
that they live His way.

No flies on Moses

46

Exodus 8 v 20-32

Blood. Frogs. Gnats.

What would God send next to persuade Pharaoh to let God's people go?

WEIRD WORDS

Dense swarms
Loads of them! Like clouds of flies!

Sacrifice
Offering gifts of food to God

Detestable
Horrible. Hated.

Stone us
Throw stones at us to kill us

Deceitfully
Tricking and lying

Read Exodus 8 v 20-24
What did God send this time?

Imagine millions of them everywhere: in your house, in your food, all over your animals, in your bed. It was terrible.

Were there swarms of flies in Goshen where God's people lived?

YES/NO _____

Pharaoh's people were covered in swarms of flies

God's people had no flies on them!

Today, God's people (Christians) are living under the same conditions as everyone else.

But Christians are God's chosen people and one day there will be a huge difference...

God's people (Christians) will go to heaven to live with God for ever!

Everyone who rejects God will go to hell, where they will be separated from God.

Read verse 25
What did Pharaoh say?

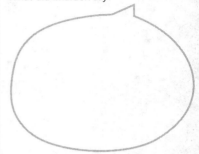

Pharaoh said they could worship God in Egypt. But God had commanded Pharaoh to let the Israelites worship God in the desert. Pharaoh was trying to wriggle out of God's commands.

Think!
How do you try to get out of obeying God? (Making excuses? Being too busy to pray?)

_____

_____

Read verses 26-32
It looked as if Pharaoh would finally obey God. Then he changed his mind again.

Pray!
Thank God that He is so kind and loving to His people. Say sorry for what you've written under Think! Ask God to help you obey Him more willingly.

47

**Exodus
9 v 1-7**

*Take a look
at the big
warning sign
on the right.*

Deadstock

DANGER–NO ENTRY!

Warning signs help us know what
not to do or where not to go. God
gave Pharaoh another warning...

Read Exodus 9 v 1-5

*What did God command Pharaoh
to do? (v1) Go back one letter (B=A,
C=B etc) to find out.*

— — —   — —
M F U   N Z

— — — — —   — —
Q F P Q M F   H P

*What did God warn Pharaoh would
happen if he refused to let God's
people go? (v3)*

—
J

— — — —
X J M M

— — — —
T F O E

—
B

— — — — —
Q M B H V F

— —
P O

— — — —
Z P V S

— — — — — —
B O J N B M T

So far, Pharaoh had ignored all of
God's warnings. Do you think he
would obey God this time?

YES/NO _____

Read verses 6-7

All of the Egyptians' animals died,
but **none** of the Israelites' animals
did! God showed Pharaoh that the
Israelites were different from the
Egyptians. They were His special
people, who obeyed Him. So God
did not punish them. But Pharaoh
still refused to listen to God or let
the people go!

Think!

What happens when God speaks to
you through the Bible or in church
or youth group? Do you take any
notice? Do you listen to God and do
what He says?

Pray!

Ask God to help you to listen
to what He says to you. Ask
Him to help you obey Him and
please Him.

WEIRD WORDS

Hebrews
God's people, the
Israelites

Livestock
Farm animals

Unyielding
Pharaoh wouldn't
back down

Boiling point

48

**Exodus
9 v 8-12**

Boils!

They're horrible.

*Pus-filled sores
that hurt and
itch.*

YEUUCCHH!

WEIRD WORDS

Furnace
A huge fireplace,
maybe where bricks
were baked

Festering
Oozing with yucky
sticky stuff

Read Exodus 9 v 8-12

Pharaoh's magicians had copied
some of the earlier plagues. But
could they do anything about
these boils?

YES/NO _____

They suffered as much as everyone
else. They couldn't even stand up
in front of Moses, their boils were
so bad!

Yet again, Pharaoh saw God's
awesome power. But would he
listen to Moses and let the
Israelites go?

YES/NO _____

The Egyptians suffering with boils
was one of the results of them
disobeying God.

Wow!

selfishness   greed

violence   poverty   war

unhappiness

all kinds of sin

**These are all results of
disobeying God.**

*But there is an even worse result of
disobeying God. It's in **Romans 6
v 23**. Find it by going forward one
letter (A=B, B=C, Z=A etc).*

___ ___ ___   ___ ___ ___ ___ ___
S G D   V Z F D R

___ ___   ___ ___ ___   ___ ___
N E   R H M   H R

___ ___ ___ ___ ___
C D Z S G

If we continue to disobey God and
refuse to live His way, we'll be
punished by everlasting death in
hell. But God gives us a way out.

The gift of God is

___ ___ ___ ___ ___ ___ ___
D S D Q M Z K

___ ___ ___ ___   ___ ___
K H E D   H M

___ ___ ___ ___ ___ ___
B G Q H R S

___ ___ ___ ___ ___
I D R T R

God sent His Son, Jesus, to rescue
us. Everyone who trusts Him to
rescue them will not be punished!

Pray!

What does all of this make you
want to say to God? Spend time
talking to Him right now.

Power point

49

**Exodus
9 v 13-26**

*Any ideas why
God is sending all
these plagues on
Egypt?*

_____

_____

_____

_____

Let's find out...

WEIRD WORDS

Proclaimed
Tell everyone! Shout
about how great
God is!

Livestock
Farm animals

Read Exodus 9 v 13-16

What did the plagues reveal about
God? Rearrange the words from
verse 14 to find out.

the	no one	earth	me
	all	in	like

There is _____

_____

_____

Wow!

God didn't have to send the
plagues. He could have just
destroyed the Egyptians. But
instead God showed everyone how
powerful He is! No one is more
powerful than the Lord!

Read verses 17-26

God warned the Egyptians about
the hailstorm. They had the chance
to get indoors, where they would be
safe. But not everyone believed God,
and so they were killed by the hail.

The Egyptian people can be split
into two groups.

**THtOhSEosWHewOB
hoELIiEgnoVErDeGd
gOoDSdsWOwRoDrd**

*Write down the CAPITAL LETTERS to
find one group.*

THOSE W_____

_____

*Now scribble down the small letters
to find the other group.*

those _____

_____

Think!

We can be split into two groups too.

| People who
BELIEVE
God's Word | People who
IGNORE
God's Word |

Which one are you in?

Pray!

*Thank You, Lord, that You are so
amazingly powerful. Please help
me to believe Your words in the
Bible. Amen.*

50

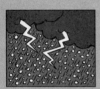

**Exodus
9 v 27-35**

*God sent a
terrifying
hailstorm on
the Egyptians
because
Pharaoh
wouldn't let the
Israelites go.*

*The hail
destroyed crops
and killed
people and
animals.*

*Pharaoh
couldn't take
any more!*

WEIRD WORDS

Sinned
Disobeyed God

**Flax
Barley
Spelt**
They're all crops
like wheat

Change of mind

Read Exodus 9 v 27-32

It had taken a long time, but at last
Pharaoh seemed ready to admit he
was wrong.

*Complete what Pharaoh said in
verses 27 and 28.*

This time I have
s_____. The L_____
is in the r_____ and I and
my p_____ are in the
w_____. P_____ to the
Lord to stop the hail.
I will let you g___.

*Did Moses believe that Pharaoh
really meant what he said? (v30)*

YES/NO _____

*So what do you think Pharaoh
will do when God stops the hail?*

Find out in verses 33-35

Things didn't seem so bad for
Pharaoh now. So he changed his
mind and disobeyed God again.

Think & Pray!

Have you ever decided to obey
God, and then changed your mind
again? Maybe you promised to do
something (like pray more often)
but gave up because you couldn't
be bothered. Say sorry to God for
those times.

*Fill in the vowels (aeiou) to complete
Hebrews 3 v 15.*

T__d__y, __f y__ __
h__ __r H__s v__ __c__,
d__ n__t h__rd__n
y__ __r h__ __rts

Pray!

Ask God to help you to listen
to Him, obey Him, and not
ignore Him.

Pharaoh was a king. Pray that
world leaders will obey God
more and please Him.

Acts: Gospel gets around

**Acts
16 v 16-21**

Let's zoom back to Acts, where Paul and Silas are travelling around, telling people about Jesus.

But they're about to run into trouble.

Read Acts 16 v 16-18

What did the slave girl say about Paul and his friends (v17)? Choose one word from each list to complete the sentence.

These men are

(A) _____

of the Most High

(B) _____ **who are**

(C) _____ **you the**

way to

(D) _____

(A)	(B)
friends **serpents** **servants**	**building** **God** **street**

(C)	(D)
telling **selling** **smelling**	**get rich** **be saved** **be slaves**

She was right! But Paul was upset by her. He knew that the girl was involved in evil stuff, and he didn't want people to connect Jesus with those things. So Paul commanded the spirit to leave her.

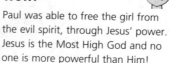

Wow!

Paul was able to free the girl from the evil spirit, through Jesus' power. Jesus is the Most High God and no one is more powerful than Him!

Now read verses 19-21

The men who had been making money out of the slave girl were furious. They'd just lost their business! They made loads of trouble for Paul and Silas.

But remember what we've just learned about God. **No one** is powerful enough to stand against Him. Over the next few days we'll see how God sorts things out...

Pray!

Thank God that whatever opposition He gets, He can easily deal with it. Ask Him to use you to spread His message to people. And to help you stand up to any hassle you get.

For a free fact sheet on *How to tell people about Jesus* email discover@thegoodbook.co.uk or check out www.thegoodbook.co.uk/contact-us to find our UK mailing address.

WEIRD WORDS

A spirit
Evil spirit living inside her

Magistrates
Judges

Advocating customs unlawful for us
Encouraging people to break the law

**Acts
16 v 22-28**

*Things aren't
looking too
good for Paul
and Silas.*

*They're in a
sticky situation.*

*Will God help
them out?*

WEIRD WORDS

Magistrates
Judges

Flogged
Whipped

Stocks
Wooden frame
with holes, in which
the criminal's feet
were locked

Jailhouse rocked

Read Acts 16 v 22-24

*and write down the terrible things
that happened to Paul and Silas.*

_____

_____

_____

_____

_____

_____

How do you think they felt?
Miserable? Hopeless? Scared?

Read verse 25

to find out how they reacted.

**Brilliant! They didn't cry or
even grumble. Instead they
were p_____ing and
s_____ing h_____
to God!**

Wow!

Paul and Silas may have been
beaten up and thrown in prison, but
they still knew that they could trust
God.

That's why they praised Him instead
of worrying. And He didn't let them
down...

Read verses 26-28

God arranged an earthquake! *What
happened (v26)?*

The doors...

_____

Everybody's chains...

_____

No wonder the guard was going to
kill himself. He'd be in big trouble if
the prisoners escaped. But everyone
was still there. Paul and Silas still
cared more about the jailer than
their own freedom. They knew God
would look after them.

Think!

On spare paper, write down
anything you're worried or upset
about at the moment.

Pray!

Thank God that we can trust
Him completely. Ask Him to
help you with the things you
have written down.

Time for a change?

Acts
16 v 29-34

Paul and Silas had been thrown into prison.

God caused an earthquake, the prison doors flew open and the prisoners' chains fell off.

The jailer was going to kill himself until he realised that the prisoners hadn't run away!

These incredible events had a huge effect on the jailer.

Read Acts 16 v 29-32

Go back one letter to complete the speech bubbles.

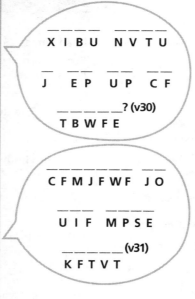

X I B U   N V T U

J   E P   U P   C F

_____? (v30)
T B W F E

C F M J F W F   J O

U I F   M P S E

_____(v31)
K F T V T

Paul and Silas told the jailer and his family how **Jesus** could save them from their sinful ways.

Read verses 33-34

The jailer had seen how powerful God was. He responded by trusting Jesus, getting baptised and starting to live for God.

Think!

Have YOU asked the same question as the jailer (v30)?

The same answer is true for you too. Have you trusted Jesus to forgive your sins?

Pray!

Jesus changes people's lives! Ask Him to have such an amazing effect on your life that your friends would want to know Jesus too.

WEIRD WORDS

Household
Family

Word of the Lord
The truth about Jesus

Baptised

Getting dunked in water to show that you follow Jesus. You go down in the water to show that you're leaving your old sinful ways behind you. Coming back up is a symbol of having all your wrongs washed away by Jesus, and starting a new life serving Him.

For more info, email
discover@thegoodbook.co.uk
or check out
www.thegoodbook.co.uk/contact-us
to find our UK mailing address.
Ask for the *"How do I..."*
e-booklets.

**Acts
16 v 35-40**

Paul and Silas are still in prison, even though God caused an earthquake and the jailer became a Christian!

WEIRD WORDS

Roman citizens
People from the Roman Empire. Magistrates were not allowed to have them beaten.

Appease
Make things right with them. Please them.

Brothers and sisters
Christians

Courage and encourage

Read Acts 16 v 35-40

The magistrates decided to let Paul and Silas out of prison, but Paul wasn't ready to let the matter drop.

What fact did he let the magistrates know? Find the correct route through the maze to reveal the answer.

H	E	W	R	Y	F
V	J	A	E	O	M
E	R	S	A	R	A
M	Y	E	I	C	N
E	Z	I	T	K	Y
N	O	A	S	P	L

H__ ___ ___ __

___ ___ ___ ___

___ ___ ___ ___ ___

Suddenly the magistrates were scared. They could be in big trouble with Emperor Caesar for treating Roman citizens badly.

But Paul wasn't relying on Caesar for help. He knew that he had **God** on his side. God is far more powerful than anyone or anything else!

God has always looked after His people. Look up some of these examples:

Exodus 14 v 13-31

Psalm 23   1 Samuel 17

Acts 9 v 23-25

Pray!
Thank God that He looks after His children, Christians.

We don't know why Paul made a big thing about being a Roman citizen. He might have been hoping that it would help out the church in that city. Verse 40 shows that Paul wanted to encourage other Christians.

Action!

On scrap paper, write down 7 Christians you can encourage and how you can encourage them. Try to encourage one of them each day this week!

Rescue mission

Paul and Silas had been thrown in prison for telling people about Jesus. But God rescued them in an amazing way. Next, Paul and Silas moved on to Thessalonica. And they didn't stop preaching about Jesus!

Read Acts 17 v 1-4

Use the code to reveal what Paul was telling people (v3).

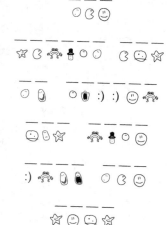

Christ and Messiah both mean the same thing: "God's chosen King". God had promised to send a King to rescue His people. Paul said that this King suffered, died and then was raised back to life to rescue people.

So who was this Christ (v3)?

Wow!

Jesus died to take the punishment we deserve for sinning. God raised Jesus back to life to beat death and sin for ever. If we trust in Jesus, He will rescue us from the punishment for our sin.

This was amazing news to people who had never heard it before! Some of them trusted Jesus to rescue them! But some didn't...

Read verses 5-9

Some people were jealous. They didn't like Paul and Silas telling everyone that Jesus was the Christ. So they got an angry mob and rioted. Tomorrow, we'll see where Paul and Silas escaped to.

Pray!

Thank God for sending Jesus the King to rescue people, just as He had promised to.

WEIRD WORDS

Sabbath
Saturday, the Jewish holy day

Scriptures
Old Testament

Prominent
Important

City officials
Important people

Defying Caesar's decrees
Breaking the law

Turmoil
Confusion

On bail
Released, but they have to return for the trial

A	C	D	E	F	H	I	J	M	N	O	R	S	T	U

Check mate

*Paul and Silas
were chased out
of Thessalonica
for telling
people about
Jesus.*

*Next, they
headed to the
town of Berea.*

WEIRD WORDS

Noble character
Good and godly

Scriptures
Old Testament

Agitating
Getting them
worked up and
angry with Paul
and Silas

When a detective
investigates a serious
crime, he **CHECKS
THE FACTS**, to make
sure he catches the
right person.

When a journalist is
writing a newspaper
article, she gets
someone to **CHECK
THE FACTS** to make
sure it's all true.

Read Acts 17 v 10-15

*Paul told the people about Jesus.
What did they do (v11)? Fill in the
vowels (aeiou) to find out.*

**They ex__m__n__d the
Scr__pt__r__s every d__y to
see if what P__ __l said was
tr__ __ (v11)**

The Scriptures are the Old
Testament part of the Bible. The
Bereans were checking that what
Paul said really did come from
the Bible.

Having **checked** what Paul said,
many people believed in Jesus.
But then some of Paul's enemies
from Thessalonica found out that
he was in Berea. They made so
much trouble for Paul that he had
to leave.

Think!

When you read Discover,
are you ever tempted to
skip the Bible reading and just do
the puzzles? It's really important
that you read the Bible for yourself,
and check that what I've written
really is true!

Action!

Do the same at church
and Christian meetings. If you're
not sure about something you are
taught, ask where it comes in the
Bible. Then check it out for yourself.

Pray!

Thank God for the Bible, which
teaches you all you need to know
about Jesus. Ask God to help you
to understand the Bible as you
read it.

Idol talk

WEIRD WORDS

Idols
Statues of fake gods

Reasoned
Argued and explained

Epicurean and Stoic philosophers
They believed in pleasing yourself, not God

Advocating
Supporting

Areopagus
Religious and moral leaders

Religious
Here it means superstitious

Altar
Table for gifts to God

Read Acts 17 v 16-18

Cross out the untrue bits below.

In Athens, Paul was happy/ upset to see the city was full of idols/noodles (v16).

So Paul told people about the real God, when he was in the swimming pool/ synagogue and the market- place/marshmallow shop (v17).

A group of philosophers/ philatelists argued with Paul (v18). Other people wanted to hear what Paul was saying about Joshua/Jesus and the resurrection/retail park.

When Paul saw all the statues of fake gods he got really upset. He wanted people to know about the real God. So he took every opportunity to tell them about Jesus!

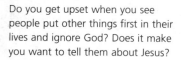

Think!

Do you get upset when you see people put other things first in their lives and ignore God? Does it make you want to tell them about Jesus?

Read verses 19-23

Paul told the people of Arsenal/Athens/Accrington (v22) that he'd seen an altar to a well-known/unknown God (v23). Then he started to tell them all about the Lord! Paul used this opportunity to tell everyone about God!

What opportunities can **you** use to talk to people about God? Maybe when religion comes into conversation at school. Maybe when someone says *"Oh God!"* you can mention why you don't say that and why God is important to you.

Action!
What will you do?

_____

_____

_____

_____

_____

_____

_____

_____

Pray!

Ask God to give you opportunities to talk to people about Him.

Why God is great

**Acts
17 v 24-28**

Paul is in Athens, telling people all about God.

Let's listen in...

Reveal great truths about God by filling in the first letters of words.

Read Acts 17 v 24

1. God made the __orld and __verything in it!

2. God does __ot __ive in __emples made by humans

People in Athens worshipped statues in temples. But God is real! He created the whole world and is way too big and awesome to live in buildings.

Read verse 25

3. God doesn't __eed __nything from us humans

4. He gave __veryone __ife

God created humans. Without Him we couldn't do anything! He doesn't need us, yet He loves us and gives us so many great things.

Read verses 26-27

5. God is in __ontrol of everything. He __ecided __hen and __here everyone should __ive (v26).

6. God wants us to __eek Him and __each out and __ind Him (v27).

We deserve nothing from our awesome, powerful God. But He wants us to get to know Him. He wants us to search for Him and find Him and live for Him. How cool is that?

Read verse 28

7. In God, we __ive and __ove and exist

Knowing God is the only real reason to exist! Most of the other stuff we spend our time on may be good, but it counts for nothing if we don't know God and live His way.

Pray!

Read the truths in bold again. Which two things amaze you most?

_____

_____

Spend time praising God for those things. Tell Him how it makes you feel.

59

Jesus the Judge

Acts 17 v 29-34

Paul is still telling people in Athens amazing things about God.

WEIRD WORDS

Offspring
Children

Divine being
God

Ignorance
Not realising they were sinning

Repent
Turn from sin

Justice
Fairness

Resurrection of the dead
Christians living forever with God

Council/ Areopagus
Religious leaders

Today's answers can be found in the **backwards** *word pool.*

daed   degduj   dereens
deveileb   dlog   dluow
edam   enots   gnirpsffo
gnisiar   nerdlihc   nuf
raeh   tneper   yad
yebosid

Read Acts 17 v 29-30

Yesterday Paul told us that God m_____ all of us (v26), so we are God's o_____ (that means ch_____) (v29). We shouldn't build statues in g_____, silver or s_____ (v29). We are God's children, so we shouldn't d_____ Him. God commands everyone to r_____ (v30).

Wow!

To repent means to turn away from our wrong ways and start living God's way. We've all disobeyed God, just like a small child disobeying their parents. It's time to start obeying God.

Read verse 31

One d_____, the whole w_____ will be j_____ by Jesus. God proved this by r_____ Jesus from the d_____.

When Jesus judges the world, everyone who refused to obey God will be punished. But everyone who turned their backs on sin and asked God to forgive them will be rescued.

Read verses 32-34

Some of the people s_____ at Paul and made f_____ of him (v32). But some wanted to h_____ more (v32) and b_____ what Paul had told them (v34).

Think!

Have you become a Christian yet? Do you want to turn away from sin and start living God's way? Do you want to tell people about Jesus like Paul did?

Pray!

Talk to God about your answers, asking Him to help you. And if you're worried about any of them, please talk to an older Christian about it.

A-tent-ion please!

**Acts
18 v 1-4**

*Have you ever
been camping?*

*Putting up a
tent isn't easy...
so how about
having to MAKE
one?!*

Paul and his friends have been
travelling around telling people
about Jesus. But when Paul arrives
in the city of Corinth, he starts a
very different job.

Read Acts 18 v 1-3

Why did Paul make tents? Paul
could have asked the Christians in
Corinth for money, but he didn't
want to be a burden to them. Paul
wrote about this later in his letter to
them. You can read it in
2 Corinthians 11 v 9.

Read verse 4

Paul doesn't stop telling people
about Jesus. Even though he has to
work, he still knows that his main
job is spreading the gospel.

Think!

Imagine you are Paul.
God has given you the job of
spreading the good news about
Jesus across lots of countries. How
would you feel about having to
make tents to survive?

*Crack the code to show how some
of us would feel.*

> I'm OOT TNATROPMI
> to make tents!
>
> — — —
>
> — — — — — — — — —

> Making tents is
> OOT DRAH!
>
> — — —   — — — —

> These Christians
> should EDIVORP me with
> GNIHTYREVE I need.
>
> — — — — — — —
>
> — — — — — — — — — —

The code words can be read backwards

But Paul didn't say any of those
things. He just concentrated on
making tents so he had enough
money to live and keep telling
people about Jesus. Are you
prepared to do tough things to
serve God?

Pray!

Ask God to help you be prepared
to do whatever it takes to serve
Him, however hard it is. What can
you do for God this week?

WEIRD WORDS

Native
He came from there

Claudius
Emperor of Rome

Sabbath
Jewish holy day
when people
rested from work
and went to the
synagogue where
they learned from
the Old Testament

61

Acts
18 v 5-8

Paul has been making tents to earn enough money to live.

That means he's not been able to tell as many people about Jesus as usual.

WEIRD WORDS

Testifying
Telling people about Jesus

The Christ/ Messiah
The King who God had promised would come and rescue His people

Gentiles
People who weren't Jewish

Blood group

Read Acts 18 v 5

Silas and Timothy arrived in Corinth, bringing gifts and money. So Paul could stop tent-making, and start preaching full-time again to local people.

*How **should** these people respond to the truth about Jesus? Put an **X** in the boxes.*

be thankful ☐

be keen to listen ☐

be abusive ☐

refuse to listen ☐

change their lives ☐

give Paul hassle ☐

Now read verse 6

*How **did** they react? Circle the right phrases above.*

They had a great chance to accept Jesus and start living for God, but they blew it.

Unjumble these words to see what Paul said to them (v6).

Yrou boodl eb
no yrou onw sheda!

Y_____ _____

_____ _____

_____ _____

_____

In other words, it would be their own fault that they're punished for not turning to Jesus. So Paul told non-Jewish people about Jesus instead.

Read verses 7-8

What a difference!

Many of these people

b_____d and were

b_____d (v8)

Baptism is getting dunked in water as a special sign that you've started to follow Jesus.

Think & pray!

Which group of people are you like? Do you hear the truth about Jesus regularly? Have you turned to Jesus? If not, don't say you haven't been warned. Your blood will be on your own head. Talk to God about this right now.

More than words

Acts
18 v 9-17

Gallio

Paul and his friends are staying in the city of Corinth.

They're telling as many people as they can that Jesus died and was raised back to life.

WEIRD WORDS

Proconsul
Local Roman ruler

Achaia
Part of Greece

Contrary to
Against

Misdemeanour
Small crime

Read Acts 18 v 9-11

What did God promise Paul? (v10)

_____

_____

_____

_____

Read verses 12-13

The Romans only allowed people to follow religions which they had approved. If these Jews could convince Gallio that Paul was teaching something different, Paul would be in big trouble.

Read verses 14-17

Gallio wasn't interested! He didn't want these people bothering him with little problems. God had kept His promise to protect Paul.

Gallio said the matter

was all just...

w__ __ __ __

n__ __ __ __ and

your own l__ __ (v15)

God used Gallio to protect Paul and make sure that the gospel could keep spreading.

But Gallio had got something completely wrong.

Are **you** making the same mistake as Gallio?

W__ __ __ __
You've learned the right things to say and even pray.
But do you mean them?

N__ __ __ __
You know loads of Bible characters – including Jesus.
But is He anything more to you than just a name?

L__ __
You know what's right and what's wrong.
But you don't always do it! None of us do. That's why we must have our wrongs forgiven by Jesus.

Pray!

Ask God to help you to have a real faith in Him, and not just go through the motions.

Listen and learn

**Acts
18 v 18-28**

WEIRD WORDS

Brothers and sisters
Christians

Vow
Special promise

Reasoned
Argued with them, telling them the truth about Jesus

Scriptures
Old Testament

Great fervour
Enthusiasm

By grace
God had shown them that Jesus had died for them, even though they didn't deserve it

Vigorously refuted
Showed they were wrong

Read Acts 18 v 18-23

Paul had his hair cut off as a sign that he was serving God in a special way. He then travelled around, encouraging Christians. Follow his route on the map.

Read verses 24-25

Apollos had many good qualities. Find some of them in the wordsearch.

- **He knew the S_____**
- **He showed great en_____ in serving God**
- **He was co_____ to God's work**
- **He had been in_____ in the way of the Lord**
- **He sp_____ boldly about God**

X	S	P	C	Q	S	E	A	P	V
G	B	D	U	L	C	O	K	F	R	N
H	J	M	Z	H	R	D	C	Z	V	P
R	C	O	M	M	I	T	T	E	D	G
E	K	S	Q	G	P	A	K	T	O	J
S	R	U	X	C	T	T	Y	L	B	Q
P	N	H	O	E	U	B	M	D	U	F
O	I	N	S	T	R	U	C	T	E	D
K	A	X	L	J	E	Y	S	M	F	N
E	N	T	H	U	S	I	A	S	M	V

But Apollos didn't understand some important things (v25).

"He knew only the baptism of John" means that Apollos didn't realise Jesus had died to save us from our sins.

Read verses 26-28

Apollos was ready to listen and learn from more experienced Christians. It not only helped him, but he could help others to understand the truth about Jesus too.

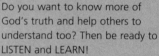

Action!

Do you want to know more of God's truth and help others to understand too? Then be ready to LISTEN and LEARN!
Which older Christians could you learn more from?

_____

_____

Why not ask one of them to spend time studying the Bible with you?

64

Exodus: God's rescue plan

**Exodus
10 v 1-20**

Back to Exodus!

Pharaoh still won't let the Israelites go, even though God has sent seven devastating plagues on Egypt.

WEIRD WORDS

Hebrews
God's special people, the Israelites

Humble yourself
Live for God, not for yourself

Snare
Trap

Bent on evil
Determined to do wrong

Read Exodus 10 v 1-2

What should the Israelites learn from the plagues?

I am the L_____ (v2)

God wanted them to know that He was their **King**. He was in control. And He wants us to know that too.

Read verses 3-6

Moses told Pharaoh that if he still refused to let the Israelites go, God would send locusts to eat any plants that were left.

Read verses 7-11

Pharaoh's officials begged him to let the Israelites go so that God would stop punishing the Egyptians. Pharaoh asked who would go to worship God if he let them go.
Fill in the answers in the grid using verse 9.

Moses said that all the Israelites should hold a

F _ _ _ _

(aka festival) to God

But Pharaoh wouldn't let them all go — only the men. He still refused to obey God.

Read verses 12-15

Imagine that! Horrible locusts everywhere, covering everything, so it all looked black!

Read verses 16-20

Pharaoh admitted that he'd sinned against God. He asked God to take the locusts away. But when God did, Pharaoh *still* wouldn't let God's people go!

Think!

Do you ever say sorry to God but not really mean it?

Or promise to change your sinful ways, but not do it?

Pray!

If you mean it, say sorry to God for wrong stuff you've done recently. Ask Him to help you truly change your ways.

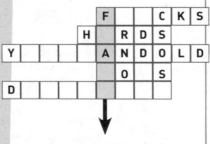

65

**Exodus
10 v 21-29**

Ever been in a power-cut at night?

YES/NO _____

It's strange being plunged into total darkness.

It's very hard to do things.

WEIRD WORDS

Sacrifices
Gifts given to God

Burnt offerings
Cooked meat offered as gifts to God

Livestock
Animals, like goats, sheep and cows

Dark life

Imagine being in complete, terrifying darkness for days.

Read Exodus 10 v 21-23

For _____ whole days God caused total darkness in Egypt! No one could see anyone else! But God gave light to the places where His people lived. Amazing!

The Egyptians were terrified. Maybe this time Pharaoh would finally obey God.

Read verse 24

What did Pharaoh say?

> Go and w_____
> the Lord. Even your
> w_____ and
> c_____ may go.
> But leave your _____
> _____

Idiot! Pharaoh still wouldn't obey God completely. He still wanted to do things **his** way.

Think!

Do you try to compromise with God?

"I promise I'll stop swearing... Except when I'm with certain friends."

We must obey God completely, doing things God's way, not our way.

Read verses 25-29

Moses insisted on completely obeying God's commands and not just part of them. But Pharaoh still refused to let the Israelites go and worship God.

We've read loads about Pharaoh and Moses. Draw lines to match them with the phrases that describe them.

| humble | proud |

| ready to do what God said | wouldn't obey God |

| said sorry but didn't mean it | kept his word |

Which one are you most like?

Pray!

Ask God to make you more like Moses, trusting God and always trying to do what He wants you to.

**Exodus
11 v 1-10**

Pharaoh and the Egyptians had survived many plagues including frogs, locusts, boils and giant hail.

But the tenth plague would be much worse...

WEIRD WORDS

Favourably disposed
They liked them!

Firstborn son
Eldest son in each family

Hand mill
Used to turn grain into flour

Hard heart

Read Exodus 11 v 1-8

What would God's tenth and final punishment be? Go forward one letter to find out.

_ _ _ _ _
D U D Q X

_ _ _ _ _ _ _ _ _
E H Q R S A N Q M

_ _ _   _ _ _ _
R N M   V H K K

_ _ _ (v5)
C H D

The death of the eldest son in each Egyptian family would be God's final plague on Egypt. Why did God do such an awful thing?

1. To show God's

_ _ _ _ _
O N V D Q

To show that God was in control and Pharaoh wasn't.

2. To _ _ _ _ _ _
O T M H R G

Pharaoh for disobeying God

God will punish people who refuse to obey Him.

3. To make Pharaoh

_ _ _   _ _ _ _   _ _
K D S   S G D L   F N

God had promised to give His people their own country — He would rescue them from Egypt.

Pharaoh had lots of chances to obey God and release the Israelites, but he refused to obey God. So finally God sent this terrible plague to make Pharaoh obey Him.

Read verses 9-10

Why did God harden Pharaoh's heart?

Pharaoh had **already chosen** to reject God (see Exodus 8 v 15).

So God made Pharaoh what he had chosen to be. Pharaoh got the punishment he deserved.

Pray!

Pray for people you know who refuse to live God's way. Ask God to soften their hearts so that they turn to Him, and live for God, not for themselves.

Lamb chop

**Exodus
12 v 1-13**

Pharaoh still refused to let the Israelites go. So God would send a plague on the firstborn (eldest) son in each Egyptian family.

But God would give His people, the Israelites, a way to avoid their firstborn sons being killed too.

Read the verses and fill in what the Israelites had to do.

Read Exodus 12 v 1-6

1. K_____ a l_____
The lamb was killed instead of the firstborn son in each Israelite family. The eldest son could say: *"That lamb died instead of me!"*

Wow!

The lamb's death is a picture of what JESUS would do 1500 years later.

He would die on the cross to take the punishment we should get for our sins. So Christians can remember this and say: *"He died instead of me!"*

Read verses 8-11

2. E_____ the lamb

There were special instructions for how the lamb should be cooked and eaten. And the Israelites were to get ready for their escape from Egypt!

Read verses 7 & 12-13

3. Use the lamb's bl_____
They had to put the lamb's blood on the door-frame. Lack of blood would mean death for the eldest son. But if there was blood there, God promised to

p_____ o_____

the house and not kill the eldest son in that family (v13).

Think!

Have you trusted in Jesus' death to rescue you from the punishment you deserve? If so, then one day God will come to punish those who've rejected Him, but He will PASS OVER you because Jesus died instead of you!

WEIRD WORDS

Household
Family

Without defect
Perfect

Slaughter
Kill

Twilight
When the sun goes down, before it's fully night

In haste
Quickly

Gods of Egypt
God would punish the Egyptians for worshipping fake gods. And He would show that these gods were useless.

68

Exodus 12 v 14-20

WEIRD WORDS

Commemorate
Celebrate

Ordinance
Law

Yeast
Stuff used to make bread rise

Sacred assembly
All of God's people gathering together

Unleavened
Without yeast

Foreigner
Someone who lived with the Israelites but wasn't one

Native-born
An Israelite

Feast without yeast

God was going to send a plague which would kill the eldest son in each Egyptian family. Yesterday we read what the Israelites had to do to avoid the plague. (Read it if you need a reminder!)

Read Exodus 12 v 14-20

Cross out the wrong words to reveal what else Moses said the Israelites must do.

This is a day to remember. Celebrate it as a carnival/festival to the Lord (v14). For seven/ eight/nine days you must eat bread/butter made without yeast (v15). Remove all the cheese/ yeast/beasts from your houses (v15). You must have a special meeting on the first and seventh days. You must not work/rest/ play on these days, except for preparing jokes/food (v16).

Read verse 17 again

The Israelites must celebrate the Passover feast every year.

It would help them remember how God rescued them from Egypt.

What a brilliant way to remember how great God is!

These days most Christians don't celebrate this feast. But they do eat a meal to remember God sending Jesus to rescue them. More about that tomorrow...

Read verse 15 again

What would happen to anyone who disobeyed God and ate bread with yeast in it?

_____

_____

_____

Wow!

They would be cut off from God's people. That's how seriously God takes sin. Anyone refusing to obey Him will be CUT OFF from God for ever. But God sent Jesus to rescue people. Now we obey God by believing that Jesus can rescue us. If you do this, you will never be cut off from God.

Pray!

Thank God for rescuing the Israelites from Egypt. And thank Him that He offers to rescue us from sin.

Making a meal of it

**1 Corinthians
5 v 7**

The Israelites
must kill and
eat a lamb, so
that God would
PASS OVER
their houses
and not kill the
firstborn son.

They must
also eat bread
without yeast.

**So why don't Christians
do these things anymore?**

Read 1 Corinthians 5 v 7

Fill in the vowels please.

**G__t r__d of the
__ld y__ __st**

That means sin. We don't need
to worry about avoiding yeast.
It's much more important to
concentrate on avoiding sin and
cutting that out of our lives.

**And why don't we need to
kill a lamb anymore?**

**Chr__st is our
P__ss__v__r L__mb**

We don't need to sacrifice a lamb
anymore because Jesus sacrificed
Himself for us when He died on
the cross.

Let's find out how Jesus is like the
Passover lamb...

WEIRD WORDS

Christ
Jesus, who was sent
by God to rescue us

Sacrificed
Killed and offered to
God in our place

Lamb	Jesus
A lamb was taken	Jesus was called the Lamb of God (John 1 v 29)
It had no defects	Jesus was perfect and had no defect (1 Peter 1 v 19)
God's judgment passed over any houses marked with lamb's blood	God's judgment will pass over all who trust Jesus' death to rescue them (Romans 5 v 8-9)

Christians don't celebrate the
Passover feast anymore. But they
do remember **Jesus' death**, which
rescued them from the punishment
they deserve.

Christians eat a special meal (called
Communion or the Lord's Supper or
Eucharist) to remember what Jesus
did for them.

Pray!

Thank God for sending Jesus to
rescue us from the punishment
we deserve for our sin. Ask God
to help you REMEMBER and trust
in what Jesus has done for you.

10

**Exodus
12 v 21-28**

*It's the night
of God's final
plague on
Egypt. Moses
is giving the
Israelites a
last-minute
reminder of
how to prepare
themselves for
Passover night.*

Final instructions

Read Exodus 12 v 21-23

Moses told them to kill the special
lamb and smear the blood on the
outside door-frame of their houses.
*What other important instruction
did he give them? (v22)*

None of you shall

_____

_____

_____

Every firstborn Egyptian son would
be killed. But God would see the
blood on the Israelites' doors and
pass over their houses.

Read verses 24-27

This night would be one that the
Israelites would never forget. Each
year at Passover time, they would
remind their children of what
God did.

So how did the people respond to
God's instructions?

Read verses 27-28

Fill in the missing words.

Then the people _____

_____

_____ **(v27)**

The Israelites _____

_____

_____ **(v28)**

They worshipped and praised
God because He was going to
rescue them. And they obeyed His
instructions.

Action!

Don't just read God's instructions in
the Bible. Obey them! Do them!

Here are some worth checking out...

Proverbs 10 v 19

Matthew 22 v 37-39

Ephesians 4 v 26

Pray!

Thank God for sending Jesus
to rescue us. Pick one of God's
instructions and ask Him to help
you obey it. Then make sure you
do it this week.

WEIRD WORDS

Elders of Israel
Israelite leaders

Hyssop
A plant

The destroyer
Whatever God used
to carry out the
plague — possibly
an angel

Ordinance
Law

71

Exodus 12 v 29-32

The Israelites have followed God's instructions.

They've eaten the Passover meal and put blood on their door-frames.

Now it's time for plague 10...

**Exodus
12 v 33-42**

*Pharaoh
finally told the
Israelites to
leave Egypt!*

Showing promise

Read Exodus 12 v 33-36

The Egyptians were so terrified of
God, they wanted the Israelites to
leave them!

What did the Israelites ask for?

_____

_____

Did the Egyptians give it to them?

YES/NO _____

Plunder promise!

Flick back to Exodus 3 v 21-22. God
had promised that the Egyptians
would give the Israelites things to
take with them. *Did God keep His
promise?*

YES/NO _____

Read Exodus 12 v 37-39

*How many Israelite men left Egypt
(v37)?*

┌──────────────────────────┐
│   │
└──────────────────────────┘

Plus thousands and thousands of
women and children too! That's a
lot of Israelites!

People promise!

The Israelites were all descendants
of Abraham.

Look up Genesis 15 v 5. God
promised Abraham that his family
would become HUGE. *Did God keep
His promise?*

YES/NO _____

Read Exodus 12 v 40-42

*How long had the Israelites been in
Egypt?*

_____ **years**

A lot of that time they'd been slaves
and were treated horribly by the
Egyptians. But the Israelites had
cried out to God to rescue them.

Rescue promise!

Read Exodus 3 v 7-8. God heard
His people crying out and promised
to rescue them from Egypt. *Was
God keeping that promise?*

YES/NO _____

Pray!

God always keeps His promises!
Thank God that you can totally
trust Him to keep His promises
to you.

God rules, OK?

**Exodus
12 v 43-51**

*To do certain
things you
have to follow
important rules.*

*Like wearing
safety stuff on
building sites.*

WEIRD WORDS

Regulations
Rules

**Temporary
resident**
Someone only living
with the Israelites for
a short time

**Foreigners
residing among
you**
Someone who lived
with the Israelites
but wasn't one

Native-born
An Israelite

**ALL ABSEILERS
MUST WEAR
A HELMET**

No helmet? Then no abseiling!

The Israelites also had to follow a
special rule before they could take
part in the Passover feast.

Read Exodus 12 v 43-51
What did they have to do?

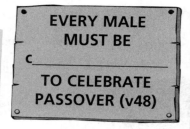

**EVERY MALE
MUST BE**

C_____

**TO CELEBRATE
PASSOVER (v48)**

Circumcision

Having part of the skin around
the penis cut off. It was a sign of
belonging to God's people.

The Passover feast was open to
anyone who wanted to become part
of God's people.

Since Jesus died on the cross for us,
we don't have to be circumcised
to show that we are part of God's
family. So what do you need to
become one of God's people, a
Christian?

YOU MUST BE
B_____ A_____
(JOHN 3 v 3)

When you trust that Jesus died
for you, God forgives your sin and
changes you. It's like being born
again. You start living for God
instead of for yourself.

Think!

If you're not yet a Christian, do
you want to be part of God's
family? Do you want to ask Him
to change your life?

For 4 free giant Discover pages about
How to become a Christian, email
discover@thegoodbook.co.uk
or check out
www.thegoodbook.co.uk/contact-us
to find our UK mailing address.

*More from Moses and the Israelites
in the next issue of Discover...*

John
4 v 31-38

It's thyme to chomp back into John's sandwich.

Er, I mean, it's time to jump back into John's story of Jesus.

Sorry, I've got food on the brain...

John: Word on the street

Looks like the disciples do too!

Read John 4 v 31-34

Jesus isn't talking about the food we eat. *What does He say is more important (v34)? The first letter of each word is in the wrong place. Unjumble it all please!*

t___ ___
o t   o d

___ ___ ___
h e t   i l w l   f o

___ ___
i h m   h o w

___ ___ ___
e n s t   e m   n d a

___ ___
o t   i n f i s h

___ ___
i h s   o r w k

Wow!

It's really important to serve God and to do what He wants us to do. Even more important than eating!

So what does God want us to do?

Read verses 35-36

What harvest does He mean?

h_____
a r v e h s t

___ ___
o r f   t e r e n a l

_____ (v36)
i f l e

That means telling people about Jesus. And those people becoming Christians.

Read verses 37-38

If people we know turn to Jesus, we should be soooo pleased! But not big-headed, because it's not down to us. It's **God** who is really behind it!

Think!

Who do you want to become a Christian?

_____

_____

Pray!

Ask God to rescue those people from sin so they start living God's way. And ask Him tomorrow, and the day after and the day after...

Boy wonder

**John
4 v 43-54**

If a friend told you that his dad had a Ferrari, would you believe him?

Or would you demand a ride in it before you believed him?

WEIRD WORDS

Galilee
The area where Jesus grew up

Prophet
God's messenger

Passover Festival
Feast to remember God rescuing His people from slavery in Egypt (flick back to days 67 and 68 for a reminder!)

Jesus had just been in Samaria. People there believed in Him right away because of what He said.

But in Galilee, people wanted to see more and more miracles before they would believe.

Read John 4 v 43-48

This important official was worried about his dying son. He'd travelled 20 miles (without a Ferrari!) to see Jesus and to beg Him to heal his son.

What was Jesus' surprising response? Go back one letter to find out (B=A C=B D=C etc).

$$\_\ \_\ \_\quad \_\ \_\ \_\ \_$$
Z P V   X J M M

$$\_\ \_\ \_\ \_\ \_$$
O F W F S

$$\_\ \_\ \_\ \_\ \_\ \_\ \_$$
C F M J F W F

$$\_\ \_\ \_\ \_\ \_$$
V O M F T T

$$\_\ \_\ \_\quad \_\ \_\ \_$$
Z P V   T F F

$$\_\ \_\ \_\ \_\ \_\ \_\ \_$$
N J S B D M F T

$$\_\ \_\ \_$$
B O E

$$\_\ \_\ \_\ \_\ \_\ \_\ \_ \text{ (v48)}$$
X P O E F S T

Jesus was criticising all the Galileans, not just this guy.

But the man wouldn't give up...

Read verses 49-54

This man believed Jesus. And his son was healed as soon as Jesus spoke, even though he was 20 miles away!

Jesus wants people to believe in Him. To believe that He is God's Son, who can rescue them.

Think!

Do you believe what you read about Jesus in the Bible?

Do you believe that He is God's Son? If so, do you do what He says? Do you live for Him?

Pray!

Ask God to help you really believe in Jesus. And don't forget to pray for the people you wrote down yesterday!

Get up and go

Ever been really ill or in hospital?

_____

_____

_____

How long did it last for?

_____

The man in today's Bible bit had been unable to walk for **38 years!** What would happen when he met Jesus?

Read John 5 v 1-7

Bethesda was the nearest these people got to a hospital. The pool was supposed to have healing powers. So, many ill and disabled people lay there in the slim hope of being healed.

But this man had no hope of being healed. Why? Put verse 7 into your own words.

[blank box]

But he did have hope...

Read verse 6 again *and complete what Jesus asked him.*

Do you _____

to get _____?

It seems like a strange question, but the man hadn't walked for 38 years — it would mean a whole new way of life for him.

Yet he **did** want to be healed...

Read verses 8-9

After 38 years, this man was healed. **Jesus has power over illness!**

Jesus has a question for us too...

Do you want to get well? Do you want to be healed?

Think!

Do you want to be healed of your sin? We all need to get up out of our sin and follow Jesus. We can only do it by trusting Jesus' power to heal us, just as the man did. Is there anything you need to say to Jesus right now?

WEIRD WORDS

Aramaic
A Jewish language

Colonnades
Columns holding up the roof

Invalid
Disabled person

Sabbath
Jewish holy day, for resting

Jesus rules ok?

11

**John
5 v 8-18**

POOL RULES
- No running
- No dunking
- No jumping
- No pushing
- No shouting
- No splashing

WEIRD WORDS

Sabbath
Jewish holy day when people rested from work

Have you seen signs like this at the local swimming pool? Boring, but sensible. These rules are made for everyone's safety.

But what if the pool attendants made up some extra rules of their own, that were far more strict?

NEW POOL RULES
- **No walking**
- **No smiling**
- **No getting wet**
- **No talking**
- **No swimming**
- **No having fun**

It would be ridiculous!

But the Jewish leaders were doing something similar...

Read John 5 v 8-15

The Jewish leaders thought it was terrible that this man carried his mat on the Sabbath.

*What was the man's reply?
Unjumble the anagrams.*

HET ____ NAM ____

HOW ____ EDAM ____

EM ____ LEWL ____

told me to! (v11)

God had commanded His people to keep the Sabbath day holy, and gave them rules to follow. But Jewish leaders wrongly added extra rules of their own — which were more important to them than the health of this man.

Read verses 16-18

Jesus is God's Son! He knew that it was right to heal someone on the Sabbath. After all, He is God's Son, so He decides what is right and wrong! And He knew that dealing with our sin problem is more important than any rules could be (v14).

Pray!

Thank God that even though we can't help ourselves with our sin problem, Jesus can heal us completely.

Son worship

**John
5 v 19-30**

The Jewish leaders were furious that Jesus claimed to be God's Son.

Today Jesus gives some amazing evidence to back up His BIG, BIG claim.

WEIRD WORDS

Entrusted
Given

Judged
Found guilty

Condemned
Punished with eternal death

Son of Man
Jesus. As well as being God's Son, He was a human being.

Use the verses and the code to discover Jesus' evidence.

Read verses 19-23

1. _____ (v19)

2. _____ (v20)

3. _____ (v21)

4. _____ (v22)

Jesus is God's Son! He carries out God's plans! He has the power to give life to believers and punish those who reject Him!

Read verses 24-30

*What's the **fantastic news** for Jesus' followers? It's in v24!*

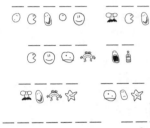

Pray!

One day, Jesus will return as Judge. Those who've ignored Him will be punished. Those who've turned to Him will have eternal life! Anything you want to thank God for?

A B D E F G H I J L M N O P R S T U V W Y

**John
5 v 31-40**

We won 3-0
last night, and
I scored all
the goals!

Expert witness

Sophie, I don't
believe you!
You're no good
at hockey!

It's true! Just ask Amy
or Nisha or anyone else in
the team...

Jesus had been telling the Jewish
leaders that He was the Son of God.
BIG CLAIM!

And like Sophie, Jesus had reliable
witnesses to back up His claim...

Read John 5 v 31-35

1. J_____ the Baptist

*Look up John 1 v 29. What did he
say about Jesus?*

_____

_____

_____

_____

_____

_____

Read John 5 v 36

2. Jesus' work

Jesus did amazing miracles to serve
His Father. All of these miracles were
proof that Jesus is God's Son. Only
God could give Jesus the power to
do these spectacular things.

Read verses 37-40

3. The Sc_____

The Jews knew the Old Testament
really well. Yet they failed to see
that God's Word was really pointing
them to **Jesus** all the way through!

Sadly, many people refused to
believe these reliable witnesses, and
they rejected Jesus. Many people still
do today.

Wow!

Believing in Jesus is not a
wild leap in the dark! We've got lots
of evidence to show us that it makes
sense to believe that Jesus is the Son
of God.

Action!

Want to know more about Jesus?
Want to find out the truth about
Him? Then dive into God's Word,
the Bible. It's all about Jesus!

For the free e-booklet about Jesus
called *What's it all about?* email
discover@thegoodbook.co.uk
or check out
www.thegoodbook.co.uk/contact-us
to find our UK mailing address.

WEIRD WORDS

Testify
Tell people

Testimony
Evidence

Dwell
Live

Scriptures
Old Testament

Diligently
Regularly and
carefully

80

**John
5 v 41-47**

The Jewish leaders refused to believe that Jesus is God's Son, despite all the evidence!

Crazy.

So Jesus put them straight...

Moses supposes

Read John 5 v 41-44

and tick the true sentences.

a) **Jesus wanted praise from people** ☐
b) **He didn't look for human praise** ☐

a) **The Jewish leaders accepted Jesus** ☐
b) **They didn't accept Jesus at all** ☐

a) **So they had no love for God in their hearts** ☐
b) **They loved God loads and loads** ☐
c) **They loved Cornflakes** ☐

a) **They really wanted to please God** ☐
b) **They wanted praise from people, not God** ☐
c) **They didn't care as long as they got their Cornflakes** ☐

Read verses 45-47
These Jewish leaders were big fans of Moses. He wrote the first five books of the Old Testament, and they knew these books inside out!

Look up some of the things Moses wrote:

Genesis 49 v 10

Numbers 24 v 17

Deuteronomy 18 v 15

Moses was talking about Jesus. These Jewish leaders knew their Old Testament so well, yet they failed to realise that so much of it pointed to Jesus, who would come and rescue His people!

WEIRD WORDS

Glory
Praise

Think!
What can you change in your life so you please God rather than seek praise from people?

_____

_____

_____

_____

Pray!

Ask God to help you understand what He says to you in the Bible. Ask Him to help you learn more about Jesus. He will! Ask Him every time you read the Bible.

Bread, crumbs!

**John
6 v 1-15**

*Jesus was
becoming very
popular with
the people.*

*Loads and
loads of them
followed Him
everywhere...*

*Even to the far
side of a huge
lake!*

Read John 6 v 1-9

1000s of people

+ empty stomachs

+ just 5 loaves of bread

+ only 2 small fish

= A BIG PROBLEM!

But it's no problem for Jesus!

Read verses 10-13

Wow!

Jesus is God's Son. Nothing is
impossible for Him!

Pray!

On a piece of paper, write some
of the things God has done in
your life. Then spend 5 minutes
thanking Him!

What did these people think of
Jesus?

Read verses 14-15

Surely this is the

P_____t (v14)

Yesterday, we looked at some of the
things Moses said about Jesus. Flick
back to **Deuteronomy 18 v 15**.

So the people were right.

But what did they want to do?

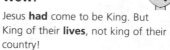

Make Him k_____ by
f_____ (v15)

They thought Jesus had come to
take over as king and kick the
Romans out of their country. They
were wrong!

Wow!

Jesus **had** come to be King. But
King of their **lives**, not king of their
country!

And He **had** come to rescue. But to
rescue them from **sin**, not from the
Romans!

Think & pray!

What does Jesus mean to you? Is
He KING OF YOUR WHOLE LIFE?
Or just someone you look up to?
If you mean it, ask Jesus to be in
charge of your life.

Walking on what! Er?

John
6 v 16-21

What are you scared of?

Circle the things that give you goosebumps.

the dark

In today's Bible bit, the disciples are in a boat on a lake in the dark. Suddenly, a storm rises up. But it's not the storm they're scared of...

Read John 6 v 16-21

They were scared of Jesus, walking on the water! *What did He say to them (v20)?*

WEIRD WORDS

Capernaum
City where Jesus preached and did many amazing miracles

Brilliant Bible Fact!

The most common command in the whole of the Bible is **Don't be afraid!** It appears 366 times. One for each day of the year, and one extra in case you have a really scary day!

Wow!

With Jesus on our side, we don't need to be afraid!

He is always able to help us, and He never lets us down!

*What have we learned about Jesus over the last few days? Flick back through **Discover days 77-81** to remind yourself.*

Jesus is _____

_____

John 20 v 31 tells us the answer. Cross out all the Bs, Cs and Zs to discover it.

C B E S Z C U S I B S T C H
E Z M E B S S Z I A C H T H
E B S O C N O C F G O B D

J_ _ _ _

_ _   _ _ _

_ _ _ _ _ _ _ _ ,

_ _ _   _ _ _

_ _   _ _ _

Pray!

Jesus is God's Son. Thank God that with Jesus on our side we don't need to be afraid of anything.

Looking for Jesus

**John
6 v 22-27**

*Jesus fed
thousands of
people with a
kid's lunch!*

*Then He walked
across a lake to
join His disciples
in their boat!*

WEIRD WORDS

Rabbi
Teacher

Signs
Miracles

Spoils
Goes bad

Seal of approval
God is pleased with
Jesus and gives Him
the power to give
eternal life

The people were baffled. Where had
Jesus gone?

Read John 6 v 22-24

Think!

Are you baffled too?

Maybe you can't seem to find Jesus,
or work out what it's all about.
Don't give up! Look at God's great
promise...

*Complete it by using the backwards
words from the word pool.*

**kees   doG
dnif   kees   luos
droL   traeh**

If you s_____ the
L_____ your G_____
you will f_____ Him if
you s_____ Him with all
your h_____ and with
all your s_____.
Deuteronomy 4 v 29

Did these people really want to find
God, or did they want something
else?

Read verses 25-27

They were seeking Jesus for the
wrong reasons.

**They wanted to see miracles.
But only so they could
be fed and get things for
themselves.**

**Jesus had something much
more important than food
to give them.
EVERLASTING LIFE!
But they didn't seem
interested in that!**

It's tragic that they were not
interested in the more important
things.

Pray!

If you've found Jesus, then
thank Him that He gives you eternal
life! You will live with Him for ever!

Action!

If you're still searching, don't give
up until you find Him. Keep reading
your Bible and keep bugging your
Christian friends with questions!

Bread time story

84

**John
6 v 28-33**

**TODAY'S BIG
QUESTION:**

*What do you
have to do to
get to heaven?*

*How do you get
eternal life?*

*Think of some of the people you
know. Tick the answers they might
give to that BIG question, or write in
what they might say.*

> **Try to keep the
> 10 Commandments**

> **Read the Bible
> and pray loads**

> **Live a good life**

The people asked Jesus what they
had to **DO** to get eternal life.

Read John 6 v 28-29

*and fill in Jesus' answer in your
own words.*

Wow!

Jesus says there's nothing
we can do to get eternal
life. Good deeds aren't enough.
We must believe in Jesus — only
He can give us eternal life!

But the people were not
convinced. They wanted more
miracles from Jesus!

Read verses 30-33

Jesus pointed out that it wasn't
Moses who gave them manna in
the desert. It was **God**. But now
God has given them something
much more important than
manna or bread: He's given them
His Son Jesus.

Pray!

Think of anyone you know who
thinks they're good enough to
get to heaven. Ask God to show
them that they need Jesus in their
life.

WEIRD WORDS

Ancestors
Their ancestors
were Israelites
– God's special
people

Manna
Special bread that
was a gift from
God. It rained
from the sky every
day and kept the
Israelites alive!

For a free e-booklet, *Why did Jesus
come*? email
discover@thegoodbook.co.uk
or check out
www.thegoodbook.co.uk/contact-us
to find our UK mailing address.

John 6 v 33-40

Bread or alive

Yesterday, Jesus told us that only people who believe in Him will have eternal life with Him.

Today, Jesus has some great promises for people who do believe in Him and live for Him.

WEIRD WORDS

The Son
Jesus

```
A B C D E F G H I L
```

```
M N O R S T U V W Y
```

Use the code to complete Jesus' promises to His followers.

1. Read John 6 v 33-36

Those who come to me and believe in me will never

Jesus is saying that if we trust in Him, He will give us everything we really need. He will forgive our sins! And give us everlasting life in heaven!

But the people think Jesus is talking about normal bread (v34). And they won't believe what He says (v36).

2. Read verses 37-39

Whoever comes to me I shall

Jesus will never leave anyone who turns to Him to have their wrongs forgiven. They are safe with Him. Forever!

3. Read verse 40

Everyone who believes in Jesus shall have

Wow!

Read through the three promises again. These promises are for all Christians — that's everyone who has trusted Jesus to forgive them.

Pray!

If you're a Christian, thank Jesus that He has given you eternal life and that He will never turn you away! If you're unsure about it all, ask God to help you make sense of it.

**John
6 v 41-59**

Yesterday, Jesus made a strange claim.

Find it in John 6 v 35.

I am the bread of life

WEIRD WORDS

The Prophets
Part of the Old Testament

Manna
Special bread that was a gift from God

Synagogue
Where people met to pray and learn God's Word

Bread and mutter

What does Jesus mean?

Read John 6 v 41-51

*In which verses does Jesus say that He is **bread**?*

| v | v | v |

Wow!

Bread is important food.
We need food to live. But we need **Jesus** if we want to live forever!
Only He can give us everlasting life.

These Jewish people refused to believe that. They wouldn't trust in Jesus.

Think!

What about you?
Read verses 47-51 again.
Do you really believe them?
Do you believe that Jesus died to give us eternal life?

Read verses 52-59

This must be really important if Jesus keeps repeating it!

He doesn't mean people have to actually eat Him!

Use yesterday's code to work out what Jesus means.

Pray!

We can only have eternal life because Jesus died for us. He gave His body as a sacrifice on our behalf. Want to say anything to Him?

For a free e-booklet,
Why did Jesus die? email
discover@thegoodbook.co.uk
or check out
www.thegoodbook.co.uk/contact-us
to find our UK mailing address.

87

**John
6 v 60-71**

So far we've seen Jesus claim to be God's Son.

And greater than Moses.

And the bread of life.

And the only way to eternal life.

WEIRD WORDS

Ascend
Go up to heaven

The Spirit
The Holy Spirit

Holy One of God
Jesus was perfect and was sent by God

The choice is yours...

Many of Jesus' followers couldn't cope with His claims.

Read John 6 v 60-66

In today's Bible bit, **disciples** means any of Jesus' followers, not just the 12 Disciples. **The Twelve** means the 12 Disciples, Jesus' closest friends.

Some of these people were only interested in being given food and seeing miracles. They didn't want to obey Jesus. Their lives would have to change too much.

Fill in Jesus' words to them.

> **What if you see the
> _____ of Man
> _____
> to the place where He was
> before? (v62)**

Jesus knew that these hangers-on wouldn't stick by Him when He suffered and died and went back to heaven.

> **God's Sp_____
> gives life. Human power
> (flesh) is not enough (v63).**

The people were more interested in earthly things: food, power, good deeds. But none of that stuff can give you eternal life with God. Only Jesus gives that. Only Jesus offers forgiveness for the wrong things we've done.

Read verses 64, 70, 71

Jesus knew that many of these people would turn their backs on Him. Even one of His twelve closest friends (Judas) would betray Him!

But not everyone left Jesus...

Read verses 67-69

Simon Peter knew the truth about Jesus!

Think hard!

Do you agree with Jesus' claims? Do you believe He is God's Son? Do you believe that He is the only way to eternal life? So will you live for Jesus or turn your back on Him? The choice is yours....

Don't forget to spend time talking to God about how you feel!

Psalms: Songs to God

Psalm 1

Psalms are songs to God.

As we read this songbook, we'll learn more about God and about ourselves.

WEIRD WORDS

Mockers
People who ridicule God

Yields
Produces

Prospers
Is successful

Chaff
Hard part of wheat that is thrown away

Assembly of the righteous
Believers worshipping God

Read Psalm 1 v 1-2

This psalm talks about two kinds of people — those who live for God and those who don't.

What word describes people who live for God? (v1)

B_____

People blessed by God want to live His way, not hang out with the wicked, copying what they do (v1). Instead, God's people want to fill their brains with God's law, the Bible.

Meditate means to fill your mind, not empty it. Using your spare moments to get God's word into your mind and heart. That's what we want to do with Discover. We want to explore God's word fully and let it affect our lives in incredible ways.

Read verse 3

What's the result for the person who walks God's way?

Read verses 4–6

What about the person who doesn't live God's way?

People who live God's way are successful! That doesn't mean they'll be millionaires. Much better than that — they'll become more like Jesus. Unfortunately, the future's not so bright for those who reject God (v6).

Fill in the missing Rs and Ws to reveal a great truth from v6.

**The Lo__d
__atches ove__ the
__ay of the __ighteous**

"The righteous" means God's people — Christians. And the great news is that God promises to watch over His people and to help them walk His way and not live wicked lives.

Pray!

Ask God to help you avoid bad influences; to meditate on the Bible; and to live more for Him.

Meet the King

Psalm 2

WEIRD WORDS

Conspire/plot
Plan against God

In vain
With no success

Shackles
Chains around the ankles

Rebukes
Tells off

Wrath
Anger and punishment

Zion
Jerusalem, God's holy city

Decree
Law

Take refuge
Find safety

Think of people you see regularly. What are their opinions about Jesus?

Read Psalm 2 v 1-6

Many people in the world (including powerful leaders) refuse to live with God in charge of their lives. They want to shut Him out and get rid of Him.

In what 3 ways does God respond to such people?

v4:

v5:

v6:

The Lord's anointed (v2) is the person God chose to rule His people, as king. When this psalm was written, King David was top dog, but now Jesus is King of God's people. Yet most people reject Jesus as King of their lives. Big mistake.

Read verses 7-12

King Jesus is incredibly powerful (v8-9). Fill in the vowels to show how we should respond to Jesus.

S__rv__ the L__rd w__th f__ __r __nd c__l__br__t__ h__s r__l__ w__th tr__mbl__ng

God won't turn a blind eye to all the evil in the world. He's given His Son, Jesus, immense power, and one day, Jesus will return as the perfect Judge. He will rightly destroy all those who reject Him (v12). Terrifying.

The message is clear: serve the Lord, and "kiss the Son" — give Jesus the love and respect He deserves as our powerful King.

Think & pray!

What is your attitude towards Jesus? Do you let Him rule your life? Tell Him how you feel. If you mean it, ask Him to rule your life as King.

90

Prayer changes things

Psalm 3

So far, the Psalms have shown us how important it is to study the Bible, live God's way and meet King Jesus.

Next up — the power of prayer.

WEIRD WORDS

Foes
Enemies

Deliver
Rescue

Glory
Greatness and majesty

Sustains me
Supports me, keeps me going

Read Psalm 3 v 1-8

David was king of Israel. His son, Absalom, wanted to murder him and take over. So David was on the run, fearing for his life.

What was David's problem? Circle the things that are true about David's situation.

> **He had many enemies**
> **He had an easy life**
> **He didn't talk to God**
> **He cried to God for help**
> **God protected David**
> **God abandoned him**
> **God would rescue David**

Prayer changes things. David was in a tight spot, his enemies all around him, hungry for his blood. So he cried out to God, pouring out his fears and asking God to protect him. Then he went to bed.

Amazingly, God gave him a good night's sleep (v5). David woke up, encouraged that God was in control, would protect him, and would smash his enemies' teeth in! (v7)

God hears our prayers and answers them. Prayer is vitally important. Because of Jesus' death in their place, Christians get to know God personally.

They can talk with Him; share their lives and worries with Him; ask for His help; and give Him the praise He deserves.

Action!

Now it's your turn. Don't go to sleep, or go into the day, with worries on your mind. Try this:

1. Tell God about your worries.
2. Remind yourself how powerful and in control God is. Maybe by reading a psalm.
3. Ask God to deal with what's on your mind.
4. Get some sleep.
5. Wake up, praise God. Keep asking Him to help you.

Pray!

What are you waiting for? Bring your worries to God, using steps 1 to 5.

Psalm 4

If you want to get in the mood for Psalm 4, put your pyjamas on.

David is talking to God just before going to bed.

WEIRD WORDS

Righteous
Perfect, sinless

Have mercy
Forgive

Delusions
Wrong beliefs

Sacrifices of the righteous
Offerings that please God

Abound
Loads of them

Dwell
Live

Good night

Read Psalm 4 v 1-8

In this psalm, David gives us loads of great advice about living for God. *To discover David's advice, fill in the missing words.*

> A_____ me
> when I call to you.
> Give me r_____ (v1)

It's good to talk to God in prayer. And when life is tough, we can ask God for help.

> How long will you love
> d_____ and seek
> f_____ (v2)

It's foolish to worship anything other than God. It's also dumb to spend our lives chasing after things like money or fame instead of living for God.

> In your anger
> do not s_____ (v4)

When you're angry, try not to sin. (Your Bible might say "tremble" — it's probably talking about shaking with anger.) More on this in a moment.

> T_____ in the
> Lord (v5)

Don't try to deal with life all by yourself. Trust God to help you — He will!

Action!

Why not make an anger plan to help you next time your temper rises. Base it on verse 4.

- Count to 10 and calm yourself down
- Keep your mouth shut
- Search your heart and get to the root of the problem
- Ask yourself if you're reacting in a good and right way
- Talk to God and ask for His help

Pray!

Talk to God about anything that's on your mind from today's psalm. And make sure you sing God's praises before you settle down to sleep tonight (v6-8). Thank and praise God in your prayers; don't only ask Him for stuff.

92

Psalm 5

Good morning

How do you like to start the day? Up at dawn for a run and a bowl of muesli? Or a long lie-in before crawling into the shower?

Read Psalm 5 v 1-3

David is having trouble with enemies again. So he starts his day by talking to God and asking for His help (v3). David says there are two kinds of people — those hated by God and those accepted by God…

Read verses 4-6 and 9-10

Anyone who rejects God and fights against His people will one day be punished.

Read verses 7-8 and 11-12

Brilliant news! God's people are allowed into His presence (v7); they are led by God in the right way to live (v8); they are protected by Him (v11); He shows them great favour (v12).

WEIRD WORDS

Give ear
Listen

Arrogant
Big-headed

Deceitful
Lying

Detest
Hate

Malice
Hatred

Intrigues
Evil plans

Rebelled
Turned against God

Reverence
Great respect

Refuge
Safety

Rejoice
Celebrate

So how should Christians respond to this great news? Decode the anagrams to find out.

Bow d_____ and
      n o w d

show respect to God (v7)

Let God I_____ you (v8)
      d a l e

S_____ for j_____ (v11)
 g i n S   y o j

There's every reason to celebrate! Being one of God's people is a fantastic privilege!

Action!

Will you set your alarm a little earlier this week, so you start your day by talking to God?
Make a list of the great privileges of being a Christian, and thank God for them every morning before you launch into your day.

DISCOVER
COLLECTION

DISCOVER ISSUE 6

Journey through the desert with God's people in Exodus. Meet Jesus, the Good Shepherd, in John. Come into the courtroom as Paul is on trial for his life but still talking about Jesus in Acts. And let James challenge you to put your faith into action.

COLLECT 12 THE SET

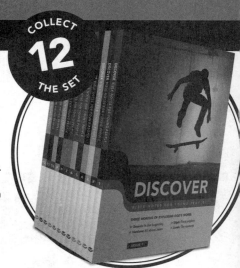

COLLECT ALL 12 ISSUES TO COMPLETE THE DISCOVER COLLECTION

Don't forget to order the next issue of Discover. Or even better, grab a one-year subscription to make sure Discover lands in your hands as soon as it's out. Packed full of puzzles, prayers and pondering points.

thegoodbook.co.uk thegoodbook.com

the**good**book
COMPANY